PRAISE FOR
Consuming Passions

"A must-read. . . . Everything about *Consuming Passions*—from the title to the recipes—just drips with Southern charm." —*Denver Post*

"This book stirs Southern characters and food into a veritable gumbo of warmth and humor." —*Southern Living*

"A scrumptiously witty memoir about family, food, and the American South." —*People*

Will West

About the Author

MICHAEL LEE WEST is the author of *Mad Girls in Love, Crazy Ladies, American Pie, She Flew the Coop,* and *Consuming Passions.* She lives with her family on a farm outside Nashville, Tennessee.

Consuming
Passions

Consuming Passions

A FOOD-OBSESSED LIFE

Michael Lee West

HARPER

NEW YORK • LONDON • TORONTO • SYDNEY

HARPER

"How to Make Perfect Iced Tea" was previously published in *True Grits: Tall Tales and Recipes from the New South,* Junior League of Atlanta, 1995.

A hardcover edition of this book was published in 1999 by HarperCollins Publishers.

First Perennial edition published 2000. Reissued in Harper 2006.

Designed by Elina D. Nudelman

The Library of Congress has catalogued the hardcover edition as follows:
West, Michael Lee.
    Consuming passions: a food-obsessed life / Michael Lee West.—
1st ed.
      p. cm.
   ISBN 0-06-018371-3
    1. West, Michael Lee. 2. Gourmets—Tennessee—Biography.
3. Cookery, American—Southern style. 4. Food habits—Southern States. I. Title.
TX649.W47W47 1999
641.3'092-dc21
[B]   98-43954

ISBN-10: 0-06-098442-2 (pbk.)
ISBN-13: 978-0-06-098442-7 (pbk.)

06 07 08 09 10 RRD 10 9 8 7 6 5 4 3 2 1

For Trey and Tyler

The day is coming when a single carrot, freshly observed, will set off a revolution.

—Paul Cézanne

Contents

A Note to the Reader   *xi*

Family Recipes

A Food-Obsessed Life   *3*

Fear of Frying   *15*

Sunday Dinners: A Memoir   *24*

The Red Kitchen   *35*

Uncle Bun's Barbecue   *47*

Dinner with Aunt Dell   *54*

Cooking Lessons

In Miss Johnnie's Kitchen   *67*

Fried Chicken: A Guide for the Wary   *74*

Shrimp 101   *77*

Potato Salad   *83*

Making Corn Bread   *89*

How to Make a Coconut Cake   *93*

Sourdough Starter Mystique   98
One-Pot Meals   101
The Side-Dish Dilemma   112
How to Season Cast Iron   122
Funeral Food   132
Chicken Soup and Other Cures   140

Consuming Passions

Old-Fashioned Louisiana Love Potion   147
The Quest for "Q"   150
How to Make Perfect Iced Tea   158
Bake Sales   165
How to Make Key Lime Pie   174
In Praise of Mayonnaise   181
Picking Grapes in August   188
How to Make Sugared Violets   192

Gumbo Ya-Ya

A Pot of Gumbo   197
Raw   206
Kitchen Fires   213
Under the Fig Leaf   221
Old Wives' Tales   226
Honey   232
The Cabbage-Eating Ghost   238
The Margaret Mitchell Bed   244
Inheritance   250
How Southerners Talk   256

Recipe Index   261

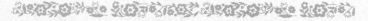

A Note to the Reader

A place very much like Dijon, Louisiana, can be found if you draw a crooked line north of Baton Rouge—the nearest "big city" to relatives who wish to remain anonymous. The names of some family members—and certain geographic locations—have been changed, due to threats and pleadings. ("If you put me in your book, I won't leave you the silver punch ladle.") Other characters are composites, mainly out of cowardice or to protect the guilty. ("Write about me *one more time*, and I'll put a contract out on you.")

I grew up in the fifties, an era when cellulite existed but had no name. In our household, tucked away in the foothills of the Appalachian Mountains, the sixties were noted for its grapefruit diets and ice-cold cans of Metrecal. My people loved food, and every meal was a celebration, even when Mama was on the famous "no carb" diet and our lunch consisted of Melba toast and a can of Vienna sausages. She always made things festive by lighting candles and playing Frank Sinatra records. During the Bay of Pigs crisis, she lugged champagne and caviar to the cellar—if the bomb hit, she told me, at least we would die happy. Every summer we drove to Nashville for the annual swimsuit sale at Cain-Sloan. As we stood in front of the three-way mirrors, she'd say, "Don't cry. In ancient Europe, chubby women were adored. Honey, we aren't fat, we were just born in the wrong century."

Many of the recipes in this book are quite elderly, like the aunts who contributed them, and they were cooked in the days before physicians understood the relationship between dietary fat and coronary heart disease. Fat, of course, makes everything taste sublime. There are two types of cholesterol, LDL and HDL. LDL stands for low-density lipoprotein; it's the "bad" cholesterol, responsible for the buildup of plaque in the arteries; HDL—high-density lipoprotein—is the "good" cholesterol, keeping the internal plumbing in good working order. As my husband, the cholesterol expert, says, LDL clogs, and HDL keeps the pipes open—a biochemical Drāno. Various recipes in the book call for butter (or that loathsome Southern entity: bacon drippings). The health-conscious cook should wisely substitute a low-fat replacement. Except for my mama, who is devoted to unsalted butter, the other relatives are savvy about cholesterol. They use a vegetable spray, such as Pam, or "lite" margarine. I myself read labels. Monounsaturated oils are the healthiest, actually reducing the level of LDL without reducing HDL. Polyunsaturated oils reduce the level of both types of cholesterol. Saturated fats are the food world's villain—they can elevate the serum blood cholesterol.

A Note to the Reader

A food obsession has one lovely dividend—it can bring you in touch with other foodies. Over the years, it has been a joy and a comfort to "talk food" and exchange recipes with family and friends. Their contributions to this book are immeasurable. I would like to thank Diana Gabaldon for friendship, *chorizo*, tortillas, and many totems to set about on my desk. Another longtime pal, Margaret Jane Campbell, generously contributed recipes, food tips, and pithy sayings. Margaret introduced me to A Southern Season, a food emporium in Chapel Hill, North Carolina—it rivals the Food Hall at Harrods. Last summer, when I returned from Pinehurst, North Carolina, with a sackful of peaches, Margaret observed, "Peaches, tree-ripened and in season, are unbeatable. The rest of the year they make good baseballs." When she recently asked for a sample menu for a baby boy's christening, I called Mama for advice. "Tell her to set the table with gorgeous, seasonal flowers," Mama said, "with Peter Rabbit china figurines strewn about. Light candles, even if it's daytime. Serve some sort of pâté, petits fours from a favorite bakery, finger sandwiches, cheese straws, a huge basket of berries with a side dish of Grand Marnier whipped cream, and a still life of cold cuts. Or prosciutto and red peppers [see page xv], but that can be messy. Oh, and tell her to serve champagne, or a tea punch with champagne, and a plain punch, too." I don't know if Margaret followed this advice, but it got Mama so worked up she had to dash out to the bakery and buy a bag of iced brownies.

John L. Myers, another friend who writes and cooks, is never too weary to discuss food. He once sent me a Polaroid of a pink-and-green layer cake, all nestled in a 1940s tin box. I will never forget his ode to the persimmon or his diatribe on Fiesta. Many thanks to Kit Sneadaker, an L.A. food writer, for introducing me to her reusable cooking sheets and for discussing the merits of the turnip. I'd like to thank Joyce Forbes, my favorite aunt, for sharing family recipes and teaching me *bourrée*; Shirley Hailstock for her chocolate cake diet (breakfast: one cup of coffee; lunch: a salad and one slice of a three-layer chocolate cake; dinner: one vegetable, any amount as long as it isn't fried or buttered).

I owe a debt of gratitude to Ellen Levine, who believed in this book from the very beginning and agreed to test my peanut butterscotch cookies and Tabasco pecans; Gladys Justin Carr for her careful editing, laughter, and valuable contributions to this book; Elissa Altman, a self-proclaimed foodie who owes me her grandmother's corned beef recipe; Erin Cartwright for her enthusiasm and good taste—two things every writer needs in an editor. Most of all, I'd like to thank my mama, Ary Jean Helton, for demonstrating the versatility of the egg and for filling my life with laughter and five-star food. Last summer we went to London and took a cab to Harrods. On the first floor, we asked a British clerk where we could find the tearoom. "Tay Rum?" said the clerk, obviously puzzled by our Southern accents—Mama's is pure Mississippi, and mine is a Louisiana-Tennessee blend, prone to twangs. Mama eyeballed the clerk and spelled it: T-E-A. The woman guided us to the escalator. Once inside the restaurant, we were seated near the cellist. As Mama nibbled a scone, tears streamed down her cheeks. I started to ask what was wrong, but she shook her head. "I'm just so happy," she said. "I have everything in the world right here—Harrods, champagne, and you."

Prosciutto and Red Peppers
Yield: approximately 2 dozen rolls

5 red bell peppers, halved,
   seeded, and cut into thin
   strips
¼ cup extra virgin olive oil
2 cloves garlic, minced
2 tablespoons minced fresh
   oregano, or 1 tablespoon
   dried

⅓ pound prosciutto, sliced
   paper thin
24 endive leaves
1 tablespoon fresh minced
   parsley

Now: Sauté the red peppers in the olive oil and garlic. Add the oregano. Cook, half covered, for about 20 minutes over a low flame. Remove from heat and cool. Lay out the prosciutto slices. Put 5 or 6 sautéed red pepper strips on each prosciutto slice, then roll into a log. Let the pepper strips poke out fetchingly. Nestle in an endive leaf. Dust with parsley. Excellent but prone to dripping down one's chin. Serve with a glass of chilled white wine or mineral water.

—*Michael Lee West*
Lebanon, Tennessee, 1998

Consuming
Passions

Family
Recipes

A Food-Obsessed Life

To a foodie, lust comes in two varieties—romantic and culinary.

—Mimi Little, scratch Southern cook and expert at love

Many hundreds of years ago, when I was a small girl, I used to eat dirt. I would squat in a Louisiana ditch, a dark-haired child in a yellow dress, busily whipping up a mud pie. Using a spoon from my mama's best silver, Francis 1ST, I added a little ditch water. Then I swooned, overcome by the color and texture of the mud. It resembled rich brownie batter. Without hesitation I licked the spoon. My pie tasted sour and felt gritty against my teeth. I ate another spoonful, dribbling mud down my chin. All of a sudden Mama flew out of the house and jerked me up by one arm.

"Stop that!" she cried, plucking the spoon from my hand. "Little girls don't eat dirt! And they don't use their mama's sterling for mud pies, either."

Bitter dirt, bittersweet memories from childhood.

My relatives spent the better part of their lives dreaming up recipes. Some were designed to lure men, and in a few cases they were made to repel them. I grew up listening to remedies for a lonely heart, cures for the blues, antidotes for colds and fevers, and how to reverse sinking spells.

Every summer I left New Orleans and went to stay with my Mississippi grandmother, who spoiled me with forbidden foods. Mimi introduced me to coffee, mayonnaise sandwiches, and bacon deviled eggs. Every morning when her soap operas came on, she'd give me a jar of peanut butter and a handkerchief full of apple slices. I would climb into the mimosa tree, propped between two branches, and open the jar. There were no other children for miles. When the apples were gone, I'd use my finger as a dipper. In that tree, I invented imaginary worlds, where elves danced under the clothesline and stole human babies from their cribs. My Mimi encouraged me to believe in these creatures. She said that fairies—perhaps even ghosts—existed at the edges of things. I saved leftover biscuits and hid them on the back porch, and by morning they were always gone. "The fairies were starved!" Mimi said.

On Sunday afternoons, when the clan gathered for dinner, my mama and her six aunts used to sit on the front porch, discussing the virtues of spinach, whether mustard belonged in potato salad, and which aunt had *the* perfect squash casserole recipe. It seemed natural that I would absorb all of this folk wisdom and food talk, but my cooking gene failed to emerge until middle age.

This is not to say that I stayed out of the kitchen—I adore all kitchens. I like the way they smell, and the way people stock their pantries. It fascinates me if they arrange their food according to the alphabet, by food groups, or jumbled together. When I wasn't lingering in strange kitchens, I was in my own, dreaming about food.

In my first kitchen, my culinary preparations were primitive. I did not sauté, braise, or roast; I heated food, either in the saucepan or the microwave. The results were usually disappointing, but I devoured them. On this cuisine, I managed to produce a fair amount of cellulite—proof that I was surviving on sub-par food.

My unusual culinary habits caused quite a stir in the family. After all, I'd descended from generations of scratch cooks. My mama was a self-taught gourmet, and I needed *Fannie Farmer* to wash lettuce. Since I was a registered nurse, some of the aunts blamed my profession, saying it had robbed me of a healthy appetite. "All of those hysterectomies and lobotomies and tonsillectomies," said Aunt Dell, shivering, as if I myself had endured these procedures rather than assisting with them. "It's a wonder she can eat anything."

Aunt Tempe disagreed. "Nursing is the perfect career for a young lady. Think how versatile it is! With all that surgical training, she can bandage burns, truss turkeys, and debone chicken."

While I had a keen interest in eating, I just wasn't interested in complicated cookery, especially if it made a mess or required long stretches of time. Like most every woman I knew, I was juggling twenty things at once—diapering a baby, rushing to soccer practice, wheeling a cart around Kroger, vacuuming, teaching myself how to write between five and seven A.M. I didn't have time to deal with puff pastry, and I *hated* sifting flour. Deep in my heart, I feared the seamy side of food: weevils, hot grease, and botulism.

And it seemed to me that good cooking demanded time. I told myself that I didn't have it to spare.

Still, I loved food talk. It was the next best thing to eating. At family dinners, we examined each dish, critiquing and consuming. *The gumbo was superb, but it would have been divine with more oysters. If only we'd wrapped bacon around that salmon before we smoked it. A stick of butter would have transformed your icing, dear.* We adored discussing pit barbecue, homemade ice cream, and how to make Fourth of July cake, which is a simple, yet eye-catching dessert: a frosted sheet cake decorated to resemble a flag, sliced strawberries for the stripes, blueberries for the stars.

Before I was sent out into the world, my mama taught me the ladylike, company side of food—a refrigerator stocked with two kinds of wine, red and white, to be served with assorted crackers, cubed pepper cheese, and seedless grapes. I learned how to throw a tea party: cucumber sandwiches, hot and cold chicken salad, cheese wafers, and a lip-smacking tea punch that called for large quantities of vodka. By the time I acquired a husband and children, I had developed a repertoire of speedy, but savory, entrées. My most successful recipes included No-Peek Pot Roast, Creamed Chicken, and Smothered Pork Chops—all borrowed from other working mothers.

After my fortieth birthday, I attended six family funerals. Our clan was shrinking; the aunts were getting old. Pieces of our culinary history were vanishing. Food had ruled our lives, dominating all holidays and reunions, lending spice and eccentricity to our dinner table. Why, recipes were like kinfolk. Mimi's mashed potato salad reminded me of a pale, plump cousin who avoided heat and sunlight, yet she always smelled of wild onions; Tempe's pecan tassies were sublime and nutty—very much like Tempe's daughters; and Myrble's lemon cake was like a flirtatious tart, one the menfolk couldn't resist.

At one funeral, Aunt Hettie pulled me aside and said, "This is a shame! What a loss!" I thought she was speaking of the relative we were about to bury, the gorgeous aunt who had left a well-nigh perfect husband to run off with a rough-edged millionaire.

"She's taken her gingerbread recipe to the grave," Aunt Hettie moaned. Then she turned to me. "Men could not resist that dish. And your own grandmother took her biscuits with her, too."

"No, she didn't!" cried Mama. "I know it by heart."

"You'd better write it down," warned Aunt Tempe. "Young people don't know how to make scratch biscuits. They just pop open a can."

"Or use Bisquick," said Hettie.

"Food is a dying art," said Tempe. "At least in this family. We're burying our best recipes." After the funeral, my mother drove me to her house, and in her sunny yellow kitchen, she taught me how to make my grandmother's biscuits.

Mimi's Buttermilk Biscuits
Yield: 12 biscuits

PREPARATION

2 cups all-purpose flour*

1 teaspoon baking powder

½ teaspoon baking soda

1 teaspoon salt

½ cup cold, unsalted butter

1 cup buttermilk

Preheat the oven to 450 degrees. Butter (or spray with Pam) two 8 × 8 × 2-inch square glass pans. Mix the flour, baking powder, baking soda, and salt. Cut in the cold butter.** When the flour and butter mixture is crumbly, pour in the buttermilk. Stir. Turn the dough onto a floured board and pat down to a ½-inch thickness. A light touch is recommended—biscuits don't like lots of handling. Using a biscuit cutter (or even the top of a child's jelly glass), cut out biscuits. Heat the glass pans, then add the biscuits (they can touch each other—they like togetherness. Bake 12 to 15 minutes or until brown.

I never sift if I can help it, and I have come to believe it is not necessary; but it can't hurt. In fact, it's bound to make your biscuits even better.
**Some cooks use two knives; others swear by a pastry cutter. Use whatever works best for you.*

After successfully making the biscuits, I decided to bake a scratch cake. I'd chosen a complicated two-layer spice cake with caramel frosting. The icing was daunting, requiring the use of a candy thermometer, but the finished product had the flavor of pralines. Beginner's luck, I told myself as I spread the icing; but the cake was cottony and dry. To this day I don't know what I did wrong. A few days later, I became entranced by a Lee Bailey cookbook. I found myself drawn to a photograph of white-chocolate brownies. The recipe called for chopped macadamia nuts, large quantities of white chocolate, and espresso powder. I phoned Mama and read off the ingredients. "I'd make this, but I don't have any espresso powder," I said. "Last time I was at your house," Mama said, "you had a tin of International Coffee on the counter. Use that."

"You think it'll work?" I reached for the coffee tin and shook it, wondering how old it was.

"You'll never know if you don't try," she said. As the brownies baked, I sat on a stool, leafing through the cookbook for more inspiration. Later, I set the brownies on a cut-glass dish, and they disappeared in less than an hour. I am sorry to report that I myself ate several, so this was not an accurate test; but I was encouraged.

I quickly branched out—homemade garlic croutons, red pepper frittata, and bananas Foster. Next, I fell in love with a set of Kmart knives. My friend John Myers talked me into buying a KitchenAid mixer, and I've never looked back—that machine is a workhorse. I still don't have a Cuisinart, and I don't have the drawer space for gadgets, but I wasn't discouraged. Working long into the night, I planned extensive menus, and then I actually cooked them. I started throwing around words like *flambé* and *sear.*

In the privacy of my bedroom, I called 1-800 numbers, ordering "exotic" items that I couldn't find at the local Kroger: capers, pesto, bow-tie pasta, thyme vinegar. By the time I started taking cookbooks to bed—to read, study, and dissect—I knew my kitchen, perhaps my life, would never be the same. I had a destiny, a food-obsessed life.

Many recipes later, I am still cooking. The food isn't grand or even remotely gourmet, and sometimes it is flat-out disappointing. Still, I press on, undaunted by my failures. I make Hungarian goulash in winter, pecan chicken salad in summer, and scratch barbecue, made in a cheap backyard smoker, year-round. If you walked into my kitchen this afternoon, you would see a cut-glass pitcher filled with sweet tea. On the far counter, under my grandmother's glass dome, sits a lemon cake with two wedges missing.

In the refrigerator, chicken breasts are marinating in garlic, minced gingerroot, green onions, and olive oil—with lots of Tabasco. Lined up beside the sink are tomatoes, zucchini, and asparagus—ingredients for a chopped summer salad that I found in another Lee Bailey cookbook. An intense, yeasty smell is rising from my bread machine. My youngest son slides down the stairs in a plastic laundry basket, then grins up at me. "I *thought* I smelled something good down here," he says.

൙ ൙

Although I was born in the Louisiana delta, I have lived in Tennessee for thirty-eight years, many of them in the Nashville area. Even though I get weak-kneed just thinking of a fried oyster sandwich, my cooking style came of age in Tennessee. Some of my Deep South relatives say that the mid-South cuisine isn't flamboyant, but it is certainly nourishing. I have raised my family on it: fried country ham, biscuits made from Martha White flour, and vegetables grown in our backyard. On an icy night in January, nothing beats a bowl of white beans and green onions, accompanied by a thick square of buttered corn bread; and on sultry August afternoons, when the air conditioner is broken and the cicadas are shrilling, a cold tomato sandwich is a tonic. This is not flashy food, to be sure, but it is heartwarming.

My boys are native middle Tennesseans, and they like to tease me, saying that their blood is full of iced tea and sorghum. This is not to say that we live in an area of old-fashioned palates. I have brought pineapple salsa to my neighbor, and she has reciprocated with a Boston cream pie. I ate coquilles St. Jacques for the first time at Justines, a defunct Tennessee restaurant that surely lingers in the state's consciousness. Once, a psychiatrist pal briefly owned an eatery in the basement of the Belle Meade Plaza, and at a private dinner my husband dined on zebra, and I gorged on hot crawfish salad.

Since I live in a small town, it can be challenging to locate gourmet items; but whenever I need an unusual ingredient, Nashville waits at the end of the highway. This was particularly convenient when I was pregnant, and subject to odd cravings. My husband, a Davidson County native, knows where to find everything the heart desires, from bagels to barbecue, from squash blossoms to sushi. It's a gourmet haven, and the home of our most famous foodie, John Edgerton, author of the legendary *Southern Food*. My mother and I own dog-eared copies of that book. We would like to get Mr. Edgerton alone and quiz him about burgoo.

Along with most Southerners, Mama and I share a deep affection for food. This appears to be hereditary. Last spring my mama was critically ill, and she drifted in and out of consciousness. One time her hands flew out of the covers and bunched around her mouth. Her lips made little smacking noises. Thinking she was having a seizure, I cried, "Mama?"

"I was dreaming about eating cake," she said, cracking open one eye. "It wasn't homemade, but it *was* Baskin-Robbins chocolate chip with white icing."

As soon as she recovered, I baked gingerbread, and she devoured it sliver by sliver. When Mama and I aren't cooking, we are discussing recipes. Every night I telephone her, and we describe our meals in lush, convoluted detail. She tells me about her roast tenderloin, stuffed with Cajun sausage and grape leaves, and I tell her about my tequila lime pie. We console each other over disasters. These things happen to the best of cooks, she tells me. We dream up recipes, then pair them with full menus. We debate the virtues of Crisco and olive oil. And we still can't decide if mustard belongs in potato salad, yet we always seem to add it. Sometimes I think we are possessed, but it could be worse. "What if you had a pug-dog obsession like Wallis Simpson had?" Mama asks. "Pugs all over the house, on needlepoint pillows and oil paintings?"

She tells me that my kitchen is an interesting place, with its open cupboards, garlic braids, and herbs growing at a slant toward the sun. And I admire her pine cabinets and her magnet collection on the refrigerator door. Her counters are jumbled, yet the room seems astringently clean, smelling faintly of lemons. She has no dishwasher, yet the sink is never filled with dirty pots.

Mama has watched me mature, from a child who sat in a ditch and stirred mud pies to a woman with a 10 × 15-foot kitchen, where real pies are baked and eaten. While scratch cakes are not always moister, they please me in a way I can't explain. Baking gives me time to mull over problems. Repetitive gestures tend to loosen up the right brain; Mama suggested that polishing silver teaspoons might be a marvelous antidote for writer's block. I do my best thinking when I am peeling carrots, grating zucchini, or rolling out biscuit dough.

Although I still rely on measuring cups, I pride myself whenever I take risks—experimenting, tinkering, substituting. Sometimes I'm careless, and the results are calamitous. More than once I have mixed up the paprika and cayenne, sending the entire family crowding around the water faucet. Another time my husband and I forgot to add ice to the ice cream maker, packing it to the gills with rock salt. When I told my mother, she laughed and said, "A nurse and a doctor! Now that is frightening."

I have come to believe that beginning a serious recipe is similar to beginning a novel—you gather the essential ingredients and forge ahead. If you wait too long to start, your butter might melt, your cream might spoil. And for heaven's sake, don't turn your back on it. A pot of water, or even a trembly first draft, can boil dry. You can't fret about grease fires, dirty dishes, or floury countertops. It's important to press on, to finish what you start; but at the same time, don't be too proud to throw out your failures.

The caveats are many. My mama used to say a watched pot never boils. This is true; however, I have let some pots catch on fire. If you keep something in the deep freezer too long, it can develop "freezer burn." If pie dough is handled too much, the crust will toughen; if you don't handle it enough, it's inedible. My Mimi used to say that dough must be controlled, gently and discreetly. It's not different, she said, from handling a man. Later, when you get the hang of it, you can mold them into the desired shape. "Show me again," I'd say, but I never learned her secret.

Sometimes, when I'm in a cooking frenzy, I leave out ingredients. The piecrust is soggy, the cake falls; I grit my teeth and toss it to the birds. I tell myself to relax, there's more sugar and flour in the pantry. Sometimes a pasta sauce is a disappointment—but I always try to rescue it, adding a pinch of basil, maybe a dash of

Beau Monde or Tabasco. Sometimes it works; and sometimes the tinkering produces irrevocable damage.

When people ask why I am obsessed with food, I tell them it's the perfect companion. It doesn't whine, gossip, or snore; doesn't pester you with phone calls and doesn't leave a ring in your bathtub. It never screams when you bite it. It won't lie, cheat, or run up bills on your credit card. You can chop it, burn it, beat it, and spit it out. Its intention never varies. All it wants to do is please the palate and nourish the body.

While I adore reading cookbooks, I am most happy when I am cooking. As I poke around my kitchen, the room seems connected to more than water, electricity, and gas lines. Maybe it is linked to all the meals of our lives, past, present, and future. In my own little kitchen, more than food passes through its doors. I come here to think and to create, to prepare meals that will join my little family around the battered walnut table. When we sit down to eat, we bring more than appetites; we bring our preferences and prejudices, our joys and tribulations, old ghosts and old pleasures. Somewhere my grandmother is hovering with a plate of hot, buttered biscuits, and somewhere else a scruffy little girl is eating dirt. Another girl sits in a mimosa tree, gripping a jar of peanut butter between her knees, gazing down on the world and trying to make sense of it all.

Fear of Frying

Whether it's passion or pork chops, anything can be fried. Too much heat toughens the meat, as well as the heart, and there is always the danger of incineration. Too little fire can leave everything undercooked. And that is dangerous.

> —Anonymous cook, discussing the philosophy of frying at The Frog and the Redneck Restaurant, Richmond, Virginia, 1996

When it comes to frying, there is one inescapable fact: Grease splatters. Anything that is messy on your stovetop is bound to be messy in your heart, too. Sometimes I imagine my grandmother's sisters, all of them with high cholesterol, cooking in front of a hot stove, dodging grease burns and oil explosions. These women didn't just fry, they fought. And every time they floured a chicken, their kitchens turned into war zones.

My mama's hands are speckled with brown spots. These are from fat burns, not age. Like a battle-weary veteran, she sits down, holds out her arm, and points to scars. "Fried chicken, 1968," she'll say, touching a scar. "Pork chops, 1993."

I can roll up my own sleeves and count fry burns; some occurred while my mother was cooking. Imagine an innocent bystander getting splattered by bacon grease. For years, whenever I got near a skillet, I pulled on a pair of long white evening gloves, bought for a prom and put to far better use in the kitchen. I wasn't taking any chances. I didn't know what it was with me and hot oil—like star-crossed lovers, we were destined to collide.

Over the years I have endured fires, second-degree burns, and melted Formica. My brother likes to tease Mama and me about our ruined entrées, meals that still linger in the collective family memory. I remember talking on the phone when I was twelve years old, absently playing with the cold skillet, dragging a fork through an inch of solid, white grease. By the time I'd finished talking, the pan was filled with ditches and furrows. I knew my mother would be furious—she didn't like people rearranging the bacon fat—so I turned the burner on high, hoping everything would smooth out. Then I traipsed out of the kitchen, into the den, where I was immediately absorbed in *Gunsmoke*.

Minutes later, my brother smelled smoke. We ran into the kitchen. Flames shot three feet into the air, leaping onto the yellow kitchen curtains. My father rushed in with a fire extinguisher, a gift from my grandfather, and smothered the skillet in one explosive *whoosh*. The extinguisher left behind inches of foam in every drawer and cabinet, which took most of the night to wash down. It also left me with a deep-rooted fear of frying, one that would last nearly thirty years.

Whenever Mama slowed down, she was a perfectly wonderful teacher. Her dinner parties were legendary, and she'd even been written up in the paper. But when it came to teaching the novice cook, she had trouble. The simplest instructions left her tongue-tied. Once she tried to demonstrate how to separate an egg, but her mind clamped down. "It's just easier if I do it," she'd say, cracking brown eggs against a glass bowl, her hands a blur. Magically, the yolks would appear in one bowl, the whites in another. I would stare, more confused than ever.

My first official cooking lesson was how to fry an egg. Mama did herself proud. As the egg spattered and popped in bacon fat, she picked up a bouillon spoon and gently ladled grease over the yolk. "It's artistry," she explained. "Pretend you are painting with watercolors." Beneath her spoon, the yolk changed from orange to pale pink, glazed with a translucent sheen.

I impatiently hopped on one foot. "Let me try," I said. She handed me the bouillon spoon. Just when I was feeling confident, a stray drop of bacon grease popped and singed my arm. Another exploded and hit my forehead. I dropped the spoon and ran. "It's only an egg. You'll never learn to make a roux if you act like this," Mama called. She was a fearless fryer; it seemed incredible that she'd given birth to a child like me. A Southerner who could not fry an egg, much less chicken, was a disappointment and a disgrace. It was like owning a spotted hunting dog who wouldn't fetch quail.

Other family members spoke up. "You'll be an old maid," said Sharon Sue, one of the churchy cousins. "You can't have a marriage without fried food."

"Men don't fry," said another cousin, the gorgeous Jeannie Campbell.

"Then explain why so many guys are chefs," Sharon Sue said.

"They sauté," Jeannie said, grinning.

The power of food is daunting to ponder. Cooks of any region are bearers of a culture and a tradition; they are oral historians, not to mention sustainers of humanity. When it came to kitchens, my Mimi believed that larger issues were at risk; if a woman didn't fry, then perhaps she was failing in some crucial way. This made an impression on my tender brain. If I failed as a chicken fryer, then I might fail as a wife and a mother. I might end up alone, rebuffed, unloved.

While my cowardice was embarrassing, I didn't think I was alone. I suspected there were other fearful fryers. Some people were probably forthright about it, cracking jokes about kitchen crybabies; others were surreptitious, going to elaborate lengths to avoid a frying pan. They'd sauté, go on a fat-free diet, move to a bed-and-breakfast, or fall in love with a vegetarian.

I began to worry. I'd been born in a small clinic in north Louisiana, and maybe they'd mixed up the babies. Maybe my *real* parents weren't Ralph and Ary Jean. My true family probably lived on boiled beef and sliced tomatoes. Ralph and Jean fried everything, even grits.

"She thinks she was separated at birth," said my mama at a family dinner.

"Not separated," I hissed. "*Switched!*"

"Honey, you're the spitting image of your daddy," said one of my aunts, looking deep into my eyes. "We know Ralph is the daddy; we're just not sure that Ary Jean's the mother."

As a novice cook and fearful fryer, I developed a new symptom: a fear of fear of frying. Some nights I would lie awake listening to the crickets, thinking the sound resembled a pan of sizzling grease. Then I'd start listing my fears. I had so many. A fear that my fried chicken wouldn't be crisp, a fear that my family wouldn't eat it, a fear of personal injury, and a fear of rickets. It seemed to me that frying was more than a way to prepare food. It was life, love, danger, and nutrition.

Alarmed, I went underground. I hid behind products like Shake 'n Bake; I collected recipes for oven fries. Years went by, and I never uttered the *f* word. There was no need. I baked and braised, boiled and broiled; I specialized in microwaving bacon, although I wasn't totally happy with the finished product. At picnics, if anyone asked me to bring chicken, I appeared with a red-and-white-striped tub of Kentucky Fried.

I longed to reform, but I was flummoxed. Where to begin? Because Mama could be an impatient woman, she used one temperature on her stovetop range: high. Random grease fires occurred, but she kept a box of baking soda next to the sink, to squelch small flames. For infernos, the fire department was summoned. At least once a month she would run out of her yellow kitchen carrying a smoking pan. "Cooking flambé again, Miss Ary Jean?" our backyard neighbor Mr. Potter would say. She also liked to cook and talk on the phone—this spelled disaster. Every other morning she would burn our toast. With the green phone tucked between her chin and shoulder, she would scrape the charred bread over the sink. "Just roll it around a sausage, and you'll never know the difference," she'd say. Then she'd remember she was on the phone, and her eyes would widen. "No, no! I wasn't talking to you," she'd cry into the receiver. "I'm trying to get them to eat breakfast." Daddy told us that she was a frugal soul, a child of the Depression, and she hated to waste food, even if it was cremated. He would stop at the doughnut shop and let me pick out something to eat on the way to school.

Mama wasn't fazed by anything. The day after a disaster, she would be standing in front of her stove, if it was operable, preparing her specialty: fried green tomato and bacon sandwiches. I longed to embrace her carefree philosophy. I prayed for courage in the kitchen. One morning, as a new bride, I decided to serve my husband breakfast. I envisioned grits, fried sausage, biscuits, and waffles. I didn't have a clue how to prepare this feast, but I wasn't worried. Looking back, I must have assumed that marriage would not only conquer my longtime fears, it would bestow instant culinary skills. I would automatically be privy to a collective consciousness, a sort of intuitive *Joy of Cooking*.

I began with scrambled eggs, something I'd seen Mama prepare a thousand times. I wasn't entirely sure of the procedure, but it seemed to involve a lot of grease, heat, and a bowl of whipped eggs. I began by frying the bacon, using a foot-long barbecue fork to fish out the charred pieces. While the pan smoked, I poured in the eggs. The grease sputtered, hissing and popping. I jumped back, and in that brief instant, the eggs turned a repulsive shade of brown, flecked with bits of burned bacon.

I served it on a Metlox platter—"Sculptured Grape," my chosen pattern. My husband accused me of trying to poison him. With two fingers, he picked up a hunk of egg. "My mother's aren't like this," he said.

"And how are they?" I asked, indignant.

"Yellow," he said.

In this health-conscious era, frying remains a heartfelt issue.

Sometimes, though, the palate cries out for deep-fried chicken, the kind your grandmother soaked in buttermilk, rolled in flour, and then submerged in hot lard. Baked, skinless chicken is a pale substitute. Your arteries may or may not remain clear by this sacrifice—you can't escape your genes. However, the food industry understands the psychology of cravings, along with cultural icons. Crisco just developed a fat-free oil, Olean. This will no doubt expose all people who fear frying—they won't be able to hide behind the visages of cholesterol, obesity, and healthy eating.

My brother is an amateur chef, but he rarely fries. He loves to grill, open raw oysters, and chop onions for *pico de gallo*. Whenever he visits, he snoops in my cupboards. "For someone who hates to fry," he says, pulling out jars, "you sure do have a lot of oils."

"I don't hate it," I point out, "I fear it." Fear it like bee stings, splinters, and tetanus shots. I shy away from recipes involving large quantities of oil. I do not own a FryDaddy. However, I have acquired a number of tongs and spatulas—just in case I ever decide to fry in bulk.

Facing your fears can make you grow. In the case of frying, you can literally grow out of your clothes. My advice is: Start simple. The easiest thing in the world is a fried green tomato and bacon sandwich. Tomorrow you can run two miles and sip mineral water. Today you are feeding the soul, bolstering the spirit, and overcoming a phobia.

First, a little suggestion: Find a calm, brave cook and ask him or her to walk you through the frying. Pour a glass of wine or good bourbon and you'll scarcely notice the grease burns. Smoke alarms are a necessity. A low to medium flame is recommended. Never leave the kitchen to work on the computer. Don't answer the phone. Your frying pan needs your undivided attention.

My mother wanted me to use her recipe for fried green tomatoes, but I suspected that she stole it from Fannie Flagg. It's mouthwatering, but it's not Mama's, it's Fannie's. My son, who is a culinary student at Johnson & Wales University, suggested another classic receipt, from the Sweetgrass Cafe in Charleston, South Carolina.

Fried Green Tomatoes
Yield: 4 to 6 servings

3 tablespoons all-purpose flour	Dash cayenne (optional)
½ cup yellow cornmeal	1 to 2 tablespoons canola oil
1 teaspoon kosher salt	4 green tomatoes, sliced
½ to 1 teaspoon pepper	½ inch thick

Mix the dry ingredients in a deep bowl. (I use a Pyrex pie plate so I can coat several tomatoes at a time.) Heat the canola oil in a large skillet or sauté pan. Meanwhile, dredge the tomatoes in the flour mixture. Make sure you get both sides, and really pack it on. Using great caution, place the tomatoes into the pan. A spatula is perfectly acceptable for this procedure, although tongs will work, too. Bear in mind that you can use the spatula to threaten anyone who calls you a wimp. Meanwhile, fry the tomatoes for 3 to 5 minutes per side. They'll be golden brown, crusted like Atlantic Coast sand. Drain the slices on paper towels. Season with additional salt and pepper to taste.

To build a fried green tomato and bacon sandwich, I am sorry to report that you must also fry bacon. This leaves a marvelous, if heart-stopping, residue in the frying pan—better known as "drippings." Next, find a loaf of good bread. Homemade is preferable. You need a bread that will stand up to the tomatoes. Next, slather on large quantities of mayonnaise. Feel free to add Dijon, celery salt, Tabasco. (Add jalapeños and you have created a fried green tomato, bacon, and jalapeño sandwich.) After you've spread the mayonnaise, layer lettuce on the bread (leaf or Boston red). Now add the bacon and fried tomato slices. Place your sandwich on a bone china plate or wrap it in a paper napkin and go eat it on the back porch. If you want to get fancy, serve with potato salad and a mug of beer, although iced tea is traditional.

In no time at all, you will be frying potatoes and doughnuts. Remember that grease is unpredictable, like a fickle lover—you will sometimes get burned. Ice-cold water is the proper antidote. The idea is to reduce the skin's temperature; otherwise it will continue to burn, and the damage can continue for several minutes. Of course, you can always wear long white evening gloves. Understand that you may still end up with a scar despite your best intentions, despite all precautions.

Some people will push up their sleeves and reveal literal wounds—deep-fried scallops, 1986; okra, 1977. Others will feel compelled to list the names of burned-out romances—Jim, 1978; Will, 1997. Read lots of poetry, substituting "frying" for "love." Tell yourself that it is far better to have fried and failed than never to have fried at all. If that doesn't work, misquote Bertrand Russell: "To fear frying is to fear life."

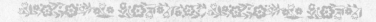

Sunday Dinners: A Memoir

Every Sunday, the whole family gathered at Mama Hughes's house in Amite County, Mississippi. They were ferocious eaters and talkers, devouring rumors and innuendo with gusto. Food was their common language, and everyone understood the dialects.

—Aunt Tempe, reminiscing about family dinners, 1991

Every Sunday our kinfolk gathered for dinner at my great-grandmother's house in the piney woods of Mississippi. Since my family lived in New Orleans, our trips revolved around weddings, birthdays, holidays, and graveyard tending. I loved the idea of traveling to another state, even though our destination was barely over the Louisiana line. Mississippi was a place of food and cousins, of running barefoot and searching for hoop snakes—a creature my mama swore existed.

I especially loved the car trip, which included a dramatic crossing of Lake Ponchartrain. This involved navigating a long, harrowing bridge with no breakdown lane and no margin for error. My aunt Dell once said that she'd watched the drawbridge heave itself open, revealing a patch of choppy gray water; a late-model blue Chevrolet sped forward, apparently hoping to leap across the chasm, and misjudged the distance. It smashed into the water. There were no survivors.

When Aunt Dell told that story, I didn't know what to believe. She was full of horrendous tales, and she collected them the way the other aunts collected recipes. Dell was deliciously quirky. She was fat and gorgeous, and she was always dreaming up schemes to make money. Some folks thought her ideas were just this side of crazy. For profit and pleasure, she had raised chickens, monkeys, and hairless cats. Although she was the most liberal aunt, she thought cussing was common, and when she stubbed her toe or burned the bacon, she'd cry, "Oh, *blank!*"

I loved seeing the relatives. When I was a child, they would line up at the end of the driveway, waiting for our car. Then I would be lifted up, passed from aunt to aunt, cousin to cousin, kissed and hugged all the way to the front porch. Every time a car pulled up, this ritual would be repeated.

When the flat, below-sea-level land gave way to rolling hills and red clay, I knew we were close to my great-grandmother's house. Estelle Brabham Hughes was a ninety-year-old, ninety-eight-pound matriarch who had never raised her voice except to sing at the Amite River Baptist Church. She loved gospel music, homegrown tomatoes, and the mimosa tree that shaded her front porch. One rainy Sunday, all of the great-grandchildren got bored, and Estelle handed out expired Sears Roebuck catalogs. "Can we plan your funeral?" asked a cousin. "I'll pick you out a dress and gloves."

"I don't think Sears Roebuck sells caskets," said another cousin.

"Well, these toy chests will work," said the first cousin, eyeing Estelle. "You're small enough to fit in one."

"I reckon I could," said Estelle.

My great-grandmother had lived through world wars, floods, and cyclones. Her own grandmother had been a child during the Civil War, and her tales came down to us through Estelle. Long before I was born, a twister swooped down and lifted her house off the foundation, hurling bricks and clapboard up into the sky. Inside the house was the family Bible, which held the only legal record of my mother's birth. After the storm, the family climbed out of the root cellar and everything was gone.

Although no one seems to recall how it got started, Sunday dinner at Mama Hughes's was a tradition. Estelle had three sons and six daughters—the tenth child, a little boy, was buried in the Amite River Cemetery, next to the river. Each of the daughters had a culinary specialty. My grandmother had grown up baking biscuits for the clan, and Minnie had a flair with lemon pound cakes. Bernice, a sister-in-law, always brought a pineapple banana pudding to Sunday dinner, and Aunt Hettie brought her famous chess pie. We were a big, talkative clan, and it took a lot of food to appease us. While the ham baked, the aunts took turns resting on the shady porch, keeping a watchful eye on the children. I preferred to stretch out under the wooden glider, listening to the gossip, which was always prefaced (and sometimes covered up) with food talk. "Did you hear about Fanny McGee? She had a tumor the size of a peach," one aunt would say. "No, the size of an eggplant," said another.

Gossip was never the main course. It was more like an enticing appetizer, or a rich, sinful dessert: You couldn't help taking a bite even though you knew you'd be sorry later. Gossip could be overdone. As Aunt Minnie used to say, "Keep talking, you ninnies. Run it into the ground!" But food talk endured. A discussion about fruit salad could last for days; methods of frying chicken could last for years. Still, all of the aunts knew the latest gossip in southern Mississippi—and even the dirt in a few Louisiana parishes. They served up these scandals the same way they served pecan tassies, piled high on a platter, passed from sister to sister. Cookies, like fresh gossip, were meant to be shared and savored, yet you must prepare for the inevitable: Eventually you run out of treats. When this occurs, there is only one thing to do: Lick your fingers and try to attract a few crumbs.

Depending on the season, the men brought quail, duck, and catfish; but mostly they brought huge appetites. They did not congregate around the women. The boy cousins brought mischief and energy; they went swimming in the river, fished in the muddy pond, or rambled in the woods; the girls gathered on the porch, taking turns braiding each other's hair or playing with Estelle's figurine collection. My aunt Dell—actually a second cousin, but no one in the family paid much attention to titles— would dart in and out of the kitchen, flopping down in one of the white rocking chairs. "It's just too hot and crowded in there," she'd say, wiping her forehead with a handkerchief. When she thought no one was looking, she'd reach in her pocket and pull out a fried peach pie, a remnant from breakfast.

I'd lie very still under the glider, listening to the metal chains squeak. From the pond a bullfrog croaked. Then Aunt Tempe would sigh and say she'd been meaning to catch that frog all summer. He'd sure fry up good. Then the talk veered back to food—

the last time they'd eaten fried frog legs, the best recipes for frog legs, and every meal that had ever involved amphibians.

Because ham was always served at my great-grandmother's house, fierce arguments used to break out over who would get the bone. All of the aunts coveted it for green beans and collards. Finally, a rotating system was invented. "It's my turn to get the bone," said Mama. All of the aunts leaned forward.

"Are you going to make collards?" asked Hettie.

"Green beans?" said Tempe.

"Red beans and rice," said Mama.

"I like white beans," said Minnie. "They're so much smoother."

"Tomorrow is Monday," said Mama. "Everybody in New Orleans eats red beans."

"That sounds dangerous to me," said Dell. "All that gas—my lord. If somebody lit a match, the entire city could explode."

"It never has," said Mama.

"Just give it time," said Dell.

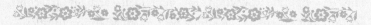

Ary Jean's Red Beans and Rice
Yield: 6 to 8 servings

Wash 2 cups dried red beans. Soak in water overnight. Next morning, rinse the beans in a colander.

Bacon or country ham	1 green bell pepper, chopped
2 tablespoons olive oil	1 jalapeño, seeded and
2 cups chopped onions	chopped
1 cup chopped celery	2 cloves garlic, minced
4 to 5 green onions, tops and	(optional)
bottoms, chopped	1 tablespoon all-purpose flour
¼ cup chopped parsley	1 cup red wine

In a Dutch oven or heavy pan, fry bacon or country ham in the olive oil. Sauté the chopped vegetables, stirring until the onions are clear. Add the flour and stir, making a sort of roux. Let it brown—do not burn! A ham bone is a nice complement, giving depth and smoke to your beans. Add the beans, 1 quart water, and the wine; put on a lid and cook the beans over a low flame for 4 to 5 hours. Stir occasionally. Serve over long-grain white rice, with French bread.

Not all Sundays were spent in Mississippi, but our leisure time was still dominated by food. Sometimes we drove to Biloxi and searched for flounder in the cloudy Gulf. Other times my daddy took me to the French Quarter, where he bought a sack of oysters and a dozen cream doughnuts. At least once a month, we drove across another bridge to Westwego, where we were entertained by Alice and Emile, two middle-aged Texans who had a summer-house in the backyard—built for the sole purpose of entertaining. The food would be lined up on a long picnic table—enchiladas, tamales, barbecue, and huge vats of boiled crabs, shrimp, and crawfish.

Since my mama's relatives lived in the piney woods, they were dependent on the New Generation to keep them on the cutting edge of fashion and food. They were especially fond of Jell-O sal-ads and casseroles made with cream of mushroom soup. Mama was always trying to introduce these country cooks to the cuisine of New Orleans. One afternoon she tried to explain how to make a roux. "Oh, stop putting on airs," said Aunt Dell. "Stop talking foreign."

"You can't make duck gumbo without a roux," said Mama. She

was a self-taught gourmet cook, a Southern Baptist who had married into a clan of Gulf Coast Cajuns—most were Catholic, with the exception of my paternal grandfather, whose Methodist ancestry was entwined with a Jewish grandfather in Mobile. My mama eagerly embraced the cuisine of my father's childhood—gumbo, jambalaya, *étouffée,* crab cakes, fried oysters. She was proud of her roux.

"I don't even like duck," Dell said. "I like chicken, plain old fried chicken."

"Dell, do you know what a roux is?" Aunt Freddie asked gently. Like Dell, Freddie was not an official aunt. She was Mama's double first cousin. She was also a marvelous cook who had migrated from the piney woods to New Orleans.

"I know *exactly* what it is," Dell said, bristling. "How do you think the phrase 'rue the day' got started?"

"Excuse me?" Freddie blinked. She turned to my mother and lifted her eyebrows. They started to laugh, but my grandmother intervened.

"I was a flapper," said my Mimi. She was the family peacemaker, adept at changing the subject, which took skill with this crowd.

"You've only told us a million times," said Dell. "Flap, flap, flap. Might as well be a screen door."

"That reminds me," said Aunt Blanche. "I found a delicious recipe for flapjacks."

One of the aunts, Tempe, claimed to be an ex-flapper, too. It was hard to imagine, because she was portly, with massive arms and thighs; she'd grab a hunk of thigh and shake it hard; then she'd sing, "Shakes like jelly but jelly won't roll!"

"Do you think we talk about food too much?" asked Aunt Hettie.

"No," said Dell. "Not nearly enough."

There were consequences to this preoccupation. Two family picnics were blighted by food poisoning. A number of brothers-in-law died in their sleep. The coroner said heart attacks, but the aunts knew better—it was death by butter.

As the afternoon wore on, the women wandered back to the kitchen. Smells wafted onto the porch, making the cousins restless. "Is dinner ready yet?" we'd cry.

"Not yet," someone would holler back. We'd crawl off the porch and gather honeysuckle flowers, pulling them apart and licking the nectar. Then my mama, or somebody's mama, would stand on the edge of the porch, her dark hair teased and poufed. She'd holler, "Dinner's ready!" We'd bolt into the house and line up at the bathroom sink, impatiently waiting to wash our hands. Then we'd race out, dripping water, and find a place to stand in the dining room.

The men were already seated around the long table in a pre-arranged pecking order. We all looked up when one of the aunts came through the door, carrying the ham on a Blue Willow platter. She set it before Great-Uncle Charlie, Estelle's firstborn son. Carving was an inheritance, passed from father to son, from brother to brother. Women, including Estelle herself, were excluded from this ritual, as if we couldn't be trusted with knives—at least not outside a kitchen. One of the uncles said he hated to see the ham sliced. It was so pretty with the cherries and pineapple rings. Too pretty to eat, said another. When Great-

Uncle Charlie began slicing, the women gathered around, their hands clasped under their chins, watching the meat tremble on the platter. As my uncle sawed, grunting with the effort, the ham seemed to bloom, each slice unfurling like a rose.

The dining table was long, with mismatched chairs pulled up at crazy angles, but the whole clan did not break bread together. Children were corralled in the kitchen, and the women ate on the run. After the ham was carved, Great-Uncle Charlie sat down, shaking out his napkin. Aunt Minnie's husband, an engineer who'd put rivets on the Golden Gate Bridge, announced that we'd forgotten to say grace. While heads were bowed, the bolder cousins snatched a biscuit or corn stick. I myself was a picky eater, but I liked to admire the artistry of the food.

"I do believe the table is buckling," said Jimmy Little, my grandfather. In addition to the ham, there was pork roast or fried chicken; potato salad; fried corn and okra; butter beans and green beans; squash and sweet potatoes; deviled eggs and homemade relish; congealed salads with marshmallows, mayonnaise, celery, pecans; biscuits and corn bread, glistening with butter.

Desserts were lined up on the cherry sideboard. Every single aunt had brought at least one cake and a pie. My own mama had fixed an Elmer's Goldbrick pie. On a normal Sunday you would find lemon chess and lemon icebox pies, chocolate cake and pineapple upside-down cake. The leftovers were not just shared, but urged upon you. *Edyce, you know how Jimmy Little loves lemony things. Take the rest of this pie. And you've got to try this chiffon cake. I found the recipe at the beauty parlor.*

These dinners defied the mathematics of Estelle's stove—there was more food than burners. In the days before microwave ovens and antidepressants, it was a challenge to serve a hot meal, much less a feast, but these women were specialists. And they had a mission. It was imperative that the men be "fed," as if more was at stake than the filling of stomachs, the soothing of appetites, the quenching of all thirsts. As soon as the last amen was uttered, the men began passing bowls, ignoring the ladies, who glided around the table, anticipating needs before they were felt.

The women ran in and out of the kitchen, tending the children, but it was rushed, haphazard care: The men were waiting. The older cousins took over in the kitchen, dishing out snap peas and spinach, threatening no dessert if we didn't taste everything on our plates. Food fights were prohibited, but that didn't stop the boy cousins from flicking beans at each other, or demonstrating the art of spurting milk from their noses. Another cousin specialized in burping, which was frowned upon by all of the aunts except Dell. We were especially fond of urging my spoiled baby brother to stick dried peas up his nose. The teenage girl cousins tried to keep peace, but it was clear they were bothered by the activity in the dining room.

"Look at them in their aprons," said Cousin Jeannie, eyeing the aunts. "Just like Harriet Nelson."

"And June Cleaver," said Nina Grace.

Jeannie shuddered. From the dining room, one of the fellows called out, "We need some more butter here!" A second later one of the aunts ran into the kitchen, her head disappearing into the icebox. She sped back to the dining room and was greeted by shouts: "Over here, sugar. That's my good girl."

"Am *I* going to be like this?" Jeannie's eyes blinked open wide. "Good girl? Is that the same thing as good dog?"

That cousin now lives an exotic life, designing intricate jewelry that she carries from Las Vegas to Paris to Greece to Hong Kong. She speaks fluent French. And she changed her name from Jeannie to Beverly.

After the last dish had been washed and put into the cupboard, after the table had been wiped and all of the men had awakened from their naps, it was time to go home. The local cousins would be getting ready for the evening church service, but I would be on the road to New Orleans. Mama and Daddy would be in the front seat, with my brother curled up between them like a boiled shrimp, the pea rattling in his nose. Mama sang, "I love you once, I love you twice, I love you more than beans and rice." Despite a Sunday supper with all the trimmings, my stomach growled. I adored red beans. The ham bone was ours now, all wrapped in foil, nestled in my mama's deep patent-leather purse. It lay there, swathed and cradled like an heirloom, something rare and beloved.

I gazed out the curved rear window, watching the pine trees give way to cypress. The car seemed to travel at a slant, into a fermented zone where banana trees and mosquitoes thrived, where the damp atmosphere held sway over meringue and pralines. Imagine living in a place where the humidity could wreck a dessert. It didn't matter. I adored everything about it. And I always will.

The Red Kitchen

FOR RENT: Furnished 2 rm. apt. near the university. Nice view. Big kitchen. No pets, no weirdos. Call after 5 P.M.

—*Herald-Citizen,* classifieds, page 7

Once upon a time, when hippies roamed the earth, I decided to leave home. I only moved ten blocks away, but my mother threatened to cut me out of the will. She canceled her tennis games and took to her bed, a wrung-out washcloth on her forehead. Just before I drove off, she handed me a jar of petroleum jelly, saying, "You'll be needing this."

"Why?" I said, a bit warily.

"Lubrication," she said. "Rub it all over your fire escape, and if a criminal tries to break in, he'll slip and fall."

My apartment didn't have a fire escape. It was on the second floor of an ancient house, carved out of the original kitchen and butler's pantry. The upstairs neighbor was a Vietnam veteran, attending college on the GI Bill. The next-door neighbors were hippies. My front door was round, like the door to a hobbit hole, and it opened into the kitchen. "I've never seen a house that started with a kitchen," said Mama.

"I like it," I said coolly. She just shook her head, then lifted one edge of a tattered curtain. Down on the lawn, the hippies had spread a blanket.

"Those men look dangerous," she said.

"They're college students," I said. "One is helping me with chemistry."

"Stop." Mama held up her hands. "I don't want to hear it."

Everyone thought I was crazy to rent that old apartment, but I was madly in love with it. I was a mere two blocks from the college, even closer to a movie theater, ice cream parlor, and cafe. True, the house was old and shabby—a firetrap, according to my mama—but I liked the wavy glass windows and the shady yard and the way I could sit on the back steps and hear bands booming all the way from the KAO house. On muggy summer nights, the tenants gathered outside, watching the lightning bugs spark in the trees, and we talked about the dire state of America: Richard Nixon, Kent State, Hanoi. All of us knew at least one person who'd fled to Canada. I felt very grown up, and I jotted down advice from my new neighbors: where to buy green tea, yogurt, books on tai chi.

Until I learned how to cook, I lived on unspeakable things: mayonnaise sandwiches, cold pizza, Snickers bars, and Vienna sausage. I ate chocolate-covered doughnuts whenever I pleased, and then I'd go on a crash diet, punishing myself with boiled eggs and grapefruit juice.

"What did you have for supper?" Mama would ask.

I usually made up a story about cafeteria food and how I'd

gorged on roast beef, mashed potatoes, green beans, salad.

Although she worried about vitamin deficiencies and anemia, Mama believed that college was fattening. One look at my pear-shaped body should have told her I was in no danger of starving. Still, she worried.

Because the apartment lacked a living room, or any sort of room for lolling about, I hung out in the large kitchen. A former occupant had painted the walls and ceiling a deep berry red. Four black-walnut cabinets hung on the north wall (the other cabinets had been ripped out and reattached in another apartment). A long window looked out into a twisted hackberry tree. In the center of the room stood a square wooden table, which I immediately painted dark purple, then festooned with daisies. Next, I went to work on the four mismatched chairs, painting each one a different color—strawberry, lime, plum, and butter yellow. I imagined friends gathering at the table, drinking green tea, which I'd already bought and stashed in the cupboard. I even imagined my mother sitting with us, nibbling zucchini bread and listening to my Carole King album.

Just off the right end of the kitchen was a tiny screened-in porch, barely large enough for the wicker rocker my grandmother donated, and a rusty-white wrought-iron table. The kitchen opened into a forbidding alcove. This led to a high-ceilinged bathroom with black walls. The tub was white, a porcelain claw foot, ringed with a plastic shower curtain; the vinyl was torn, but it was color coordinated, printed with ebony seashells and seahorses. Periodically I filled the tub with ice and Budweiser, inviting everyone I knew. The hippies brought Lay's chips and onion dip. The veteran produced a Melanie album. My friends brought fondue and gossip. When the party ended, I reached down into the icy tub and pulled the rubber stopper. All night long, as the ice melted, the cubes shifted and collided and slowly trickled down the ancient drain.

"A black bathroom," my mama said the first time she saw it, she clapped one hand over her mouth. "And that tub. I don't think there's enough bleach in the world to clean it." Later, she described the room to my grandmother as "tomblike." She thought my bedroom was claustrophobic, and it was rather tiny. It had been carved out of the former butler's pantry; when I wanted to open the closet, I had to push the bed away from the wall, ease open the door, and then squeeze through the narrow opening. Mama donated her Frank Sinatra poster to hang over my bed. "He'll go perfect with those creatures you like so much," she said, nodding at a Rolling Stones poster. "Frank's a nice balance."

The front door had no bell or knocker, but I was fortunate to have good neighbors. The hippies presented me with a hand-painted gourd—canary yellow, painted with peace symbols. It rattled ever so slightly when I shook it. The Vietnam veteran taught everyone in the building how to make burning roses—shake two drops Tabasco into one jigger tequila and a rose will take shape.

When it became clear that I wasn't giving up the apartment, Mama gave me a metal colander, which I have to this day, and a bag of apples from her tree. Mimi produced an electric skillet and a sackful of garden tomatoes. Both women thought I'd lost my mind to live in a great big kitchen. True, they loved to eat and cook, but where was I supposed to *sit*? Where could I comfortably watch TV?

In truth, I'd been seduced by the quaint screened-in porch, and my mama knew it. "You'll get to use it for five, maybe six months," she prophesied. "Have you forgotten these cold Tennessee winters?"

"I've never seen a room with a red ceiling," said my grandmother (her kitchen was pink and white).

"I have," said Mama, nodding gravely. "In the French Quarter. And the rats were so big they ran off with the traps."

"I haven't seen any rats," I said.

"Just you wait," said Mama.

"Would you-all like something to drink?" I said, finally remembering my manners. I reached up into the cabinet, ignoring the tin of green tea, and pulled out a box of Lipton. I lifted a bag by the string and watched it dangle. Never in my life had I made iced tea. I had never even watched my mama make it. The iced tea just seemed to appear every afternoon at five o'clock, in a cut-glass pitcher.

"Where's your kettle?" asked Mama, poking into a cupboard. I hunkered down, reaching into a murky cabinet that was lined with apple-red shelf paper; I pulled out a battered saucepan.

"No kettle? Didn't I give you one? Do you have a lid?" She frowned at the pan. After rinsing it out twice, she filled it with cold tap water, then set it on the burner. While I rummaged for a lid, Mama opened the Lipton box and pulled out four tea bags. My grandmother walked over to the sink and began peeling apples. "Do you have any cinnamon?" she asked. I opened a cabinet, stood on my toes, and grabbed a small tin. It has always been my belief that you can size up people by the way they assemble food. I have known crazy women who organized cans by color. And one zany fellow arranged his pantry by the size of cans and packages. I myself like to categorize by food groups.

"What are you fixing?" Mama asked Mimi. Leaning against the sink, she bit into an apple peel and chewed thoughtfully.

"Applesauce," said Mimi, eyeing me. "Easy to make, easy to digest. And once you learn how to fix it, you'll never starve."

Mimi's Applesauce
Yield: 4 servings

8 apples	½ teaspoon ground
½ cup apple cider	cinnamon
4 tablespoons unsalted	1 teaspoon fresh lemon
butter	juice
2 to 5 tablespoons sugar	

Peel and cut the apples into chunks. Put in a saucepan with apple cider, butter, sugar, cinnamon, and lemon juice. Sometimes I use white sugar, other times a blend of white and brown; honey is an admirable substitute. Don't be afraid to experiment. You have to work hard to hurt this recipe. Cook the apples on a low flame for 25 to 30 minutes, or until the liquid is absorbed and the apples are tender and mushy. If you don't like lumpy applesauce, run the mixture through a food mill. Sometimes Mimi added a handful of red-hot candies, stirring on low heat until the confection melted and the sauce turned a fierce shade of red. "Children are extremely partial to candied applesauce," she used to say.

Around mid-June, Aunt Dell drove up for a lengthy visit. She brought brownies, and we ate them at the purple table. She thought all front doors should open into kitchens. "Living rooms are overrated," she said, licking chocolate icing from her fingers. "In fact, I use mine for storage."

This was true. Back in Louisiana, Dell's parlor was filled with hairless cats, old *Saturday Evening Posts*, neatly folded Winn-Dixie sacks, and Grecian statues. The statues were used as wig stands and cat perches.

Since Dell was in town, I decided to have a dinner party. This was before the days of carrot stick and cauliflower dippers, before the days of salsa. Chips and dip were a dominant feature at all the parties I attended. Nobody under thirty knew how to cook a full meal, so I felt confident about my little party. I invited the hippies, who asked if they could bring anything. I hadn't given a thought to the menu, but I said, "Dessert?"

"Dig it," they said. "We'll bring Sara Lee. And don't worry. Cook whatever turns you on. We're not vegans or anything."

Aunt Dell, who'd been eavesdropping, said she sure hoped my dinner guests weren't on drugs—or worse, escaped mental patients. "Vegan?" she said, mulling over the word. "Or vague-and? What does it mean?"

I didn't know. The hippies seemed quite normal to me. The taller one, Mitchell, was a physics major. He had a thick, black beard and wore leather bracelets; the short guy, Cary, was majoring in chemistry. He had shiny red hair, which he pulled into a long ponytail. This was about twenty years before ponytails were fashionable for men—it was the age of long, stringy hair, headbands, and afros. He had gorgeous blue eyes that stared out of round, wire-rimmed glasses, and he had a Yankee accent.

"They could be Vulcans," Dell said, biting her nails.

"I don't think so," I told her. "The other day they brought me supper. Eggplant Parmesan."

"Was it good?" Dell leaned forward.

"Mouthwatering," I said.

"Then you'll have to reciprocate with something fabulous," she said. She opened the front door, dashed out to her car, and opened the trunk, riffling through papers. She returned with a recipe file. "Here you go," she said, handing me an index card. "A no-fail rice and pork chop casserole. You can fix that for your hippies."

I blinked at the card, which was creased and yellowed. The main ingredients were canned soups—cream of celery and mushroom— topped with French-fried onion rings. Dell swore up and down that it was foolproof, something a cross-eyed monkey could prepare. I looked far into the future: I saw myself in a modern kitchen, roasting beef bones. But my oven was old, with a finicky thermostat; and I'd substituted extra-long-grain rice for the Minute rice.

The hippies brought Sara Lee cheesecake, which I set on the counter to defrost. I scurried around lighting dimestore candles. They flickered on the counters and the purple table, casting long shadows toward the red ceiling. "You-all are real hippies?" Dell said. "Not that I'm against them or anything."

"We don't like labels," said Mitchell, fingering his leather bracelets.

" 'Hippie' is a term used by non-hippies," said Cary.

"We're heads," said Mitchell.

"Oh," said Dell, looking puzzled, then alarmed.

We all sat down. As I dished up the casserole, I saw that something had gone wrong. The rice looked peculiar, and it had stuck to the bottom of the pan. Dell took a bite and her face contorted.

"Too hot?" I said hopefully.

"No!" Dell cradled her jaw. "The rice is raw. I think I chipped a molar."

"You said a cross-eyed monkey could fix this," I cried.

"I guess not," Dell muttered under her breath.

"Let's just eat the cheesecake," said Cary.

"I've got green-onion dip in the fridge," I said.

"Dig it," said Mitchell.

The next day my grandmother came over with her famous 7-UP Cake. "You'll make mistakes," she said, patting my head. "But don't let that stop you. Just keep practicing."

"But I could have broken their teeth," I wailed.

"At least you didn't poison them," she said. "Even *I* have done that a time or two. Not on purpose, mind you. So, honey, please don't fret. Cooks are only human."

"But what did I do wrong, Mimi?"

"Next time, don't use one of Dell's recipes."

That summer I taught myself to cook in the red kitchen. My mother gave me a yard-sale copy of *Better Homes and Gardens Cookbook* and Mimi offered her battered and stained *River Road*. I studied the books, then walked to the market, shopping with a fierce exhilaration. Determined to use my senses, I picked up a whole broccoli, gazing at the florets with a feverish intensity. It smelled like summers in a damp Florida town, where the tap water gave off a sulfuric odor. It was the color of a wild parrot, hiding in a palmetto, and it called out my name. I *had* to have it. Mama's cookbook had suggested that broccoli was *delicious as a vegetable accompaniment or cold with a vinaigrette*. I had no idea what that meant, or what I should do with the broccoli, but its appearance was enticing, even if its odor was repellent—with a tinge of nastiness. Perhaps Eve had been drawn to broccoli in Eden. A forbidden vegetable as opposed to a forbidden fruit. I pondered this, moving slowly down the produce aisle, searching for the thinnest stalks of asparagus, the plumpest grapes, the ripest avocados.

I spent all of my money on chicken breasts, lemons, dried herbs. If a dish failed, I cooked it over and over until I got it right. I didn't produce anything exceptional, but I was never hungry. While I baked potatoes and cupcakes, I dreamed of having a beautiful kitchen someday. It would have windows everywhere, with sun pouring through the panes like strained lemon juice. I would paint the ceiling blue, with clouds and red birds. I would learn the art of proportion, and how to reduce recipes. I would own plenty of tea towels, a jar for cookies; my counters would shine, gathering up all the light in the world and throwing it back. It was a memorable summer in a memorable kitchen, that one season of self-reliance.

Sometimes I dream about my red kitchen and those tentative meals I prepared. I cooked in earnest, and in ignorance, but I never lacked for company. Sometimes Dell drove up, and Mama and Mimi were always dropping by with casseroles; then they'd snoop around, looking for evidence of what Mama called "overnight entertaining." Mama was vehemently opposed to the sexual revolution.

Now, twenty-five years later, I still live in an old house, near a bustling, loud university, where the band practices "Star Wars" and "New York, New York." I still don't have enough cabinet space, but I have two big windows, filled with herbs and experimental vinegars. A pot rack holds the overflow. When we were renovating, we knocked out a wall, turning the sunporch into a breakfast room. The room has no heat or air-conditioning—which makes it the perfect place to let rolls rise in the summer, and the best place to store potatoes and geraniums in the winter.

My front door opens into a proper living room—a junk-store French sofa, covered in a lurid shade of pink, and deep-silled windows where the cat likes to perch. The other day Mama was visiting, and I said, "If only I'd done away with a living room. If only I'd made this a red kitchen."

"I don't know about red," said Mama, "but a house should start with a kitchen. You should step right into it."

Even when I'm all by myself, I never cook alone. My grandparents are dead, along with my father and some favorite aunts. Dell disappeared into the wilds of Florida. But my family lives on in their recipes. I bring Mimi's chocolate cake to potlucks and Aunt Tempe's majestic coconut layer cake to holiday parties. I make Aunt Blanche's pancakes on Sunday mornings. The aunts, living and dead, left me with a legacy of food—and the confidence to cook it. Whenever I smell apples, I think of Mimi peeling winesaps in my old red kitchen. The memory of Dell goads me into serving experimental entrées to hapless guests. Whenever I'm making biscuits, cutting them out with a child's jelly glass, I feel my grandmother hovering. She is somewhere over the pot rack, telling me that biscuits are like cats, they don't take to handling.

"Am I doing this right?" I ask her.

"You're doing just fine," she says. "Don't let me stop you."

Uncle Bun's Barbecue

Barbecue is part of our family history—it is a cautionary tale, a story of how love can char and blacken, and how the sweetest, most innocent heart can burn to ash.

—Ary Jean Helton, gourmet cook and chronicler of family romances, 1958

Long before my great-great-uncle Bun went to Brazil and married the South American nymphomaniac, he made legendary barbecue. This was in the 1930s, in Tangipahoa Parish, near Independence, Louisiana. Uncle Bernice—known to everyone as Bun—owned a barbecue pit. He also ran a roadside motel, a cafe, and, farther down the road, a fishing camp. But it was the barbecue that drew the locals.

The pit was located on Highway 51, better known as the Swamp Road. It was a dangerous highway, low and dippy, lined with ditches. One thing was certain—you didn't want to have car trouble on this road, because the ditches were full of snakes and Lord knew what else. When you reached La Plas, the road divided. If you turned left, you'd end up in New Orleans; if you turned right, you'd drive into Baton Rouge. Day or night you could see cars whirring by the old barbecue pit. The motorists drove with the windows down, and the smell of blackened meat filled them with all sorts of longings. They would often turn around, backtracking to Uncle Bun's, and order a pork platter with potato salad, slaw, baked beans, and corn bread.

Bun was fanatical about his hickory fire. All during the night, he'd crawl out of bed and trudge over to the pit, adding chunks of hickory, sweetening the coals with pecan and apple wood. The smokehouse was separate from his restaurant. The pit was a small concrete-and-brick building at the end of an oyster-shell path. Behind the restaurant and the pit, set way back in the piney woods, stood a white frame house with two deep porches. For many years, he'd lived in that house with his mother, Mrs. Felder, who made her famous whipped-cream cake every Friday and sold it at the restaurant. Bun and his mama also owned a fishing camp in Manchack, Louisiana, featuring a screened-in restaurant that looked out on the lake and a long wooden pier.

With so much going on, he didn't seem to notice that his South American bride had worn out three sets of tires; she was forever driving up and down the Swamp Road. The aunts thought she ran around with no-account men, but no one could prove anything. Besides, Bun loved her so much it wouldn't have mattered. The family couldn't understand why a talented man like Bun would marry a loose woman. In addition to being a pit master, Uncle Bun was also an ironworker. He had met the nympho on a trip to Brazil. As he walked down the street, he spotted a beautiful woman sitting in a window, waving at him. She had short black hair that curled around her face. She kept waving. According to family legend, the woman was luring Bun into a house of ill repute—or, as Mama said, a house of ill "repoot." In any event, Uncle Bun fell in love on the spot. When he returned to Louisiana, he had the tiny brunette on his arm. "This is Sidone, my bride," he told the family. Mrs. Felder took to her bed and stayed there for the better part of a decade; but the other relatives took Sidone in stride—until the rumors began.

One summer afternoon, the nymphomaniac agreed to baby-sit my mother. As soon as my grandparents drove off, heading toward Baton Rouge, Sidone dragged Mama toward the motor court and pushed her into a seedy little room. Then she locked the door, heartlessly ignoring my mama's cries. A while later, my mama heard a car start up. She guessed it was Sidone, disappearing on one of her mysterious trips, but it was hard to be certain. The restaurant generated a fair amount of traffic. Also, Mama was short for a six-year-old, and the bathroom window was high and unreachable. For an immeasurable time, Mama sat on the bed and fumed until Sidone came back and unlocked the door. Mama took off running, and she collided with Uncle Bun, bouncing off his aproned stomach.

"Anything wrong, Ary Jean?" he asked, looking at her with surprise. Normally Mama wasn't a crybaby; she was tough.

"Nothing is wrong," Sidone said quickly, glaring at Mama. "Tell him you're being silly."

"Well, get you some barbecue," Bun said. "That'll cure the sillies."

Except for Uncle Bun, the entire family knew about Sidone's excursions. She would tell Bun she was going to Baton Rouge to buy fabric, and she'd come home covered in hickeys. "Don't you think that's just a little strange, Bernice?" said Mrs. Felder from her sickbed.

"All women like to shop," he said.

"She's going to drive you crazy," said Mrs. Felder. "Stark, raving mad."

Years later, this prediction came true. Late one afternoon, my granddaddy got a phone call. "Jimmy Little," the caller said, "your uncle Bun has gone crazy. You need to get down here quick."

My grandfather drove to Independence and found Uncle Bun in the pit house, stoking the fire. "I have forgotten my sauce recipe, Jimmy," he cried. "It's gone."

Sidone stood in the doorway, eyeing my grandfather. He was a handsome young man, with blue eyes and thick auburn hair. In later years, he was a dead ringer for Dana Andrews in *The Purple Heart*. "My sauce is missing!" wailed Bun.

"That's not all that's gone," said Sidone, tapping one tiny finger against her temple.

My grandfather consulted with the family, and Bun was taken to a private institution. "He's either had a stroke or he's lost his mind," said Aunt Minnie.

"No, Sidone drove him crazy," said Mimi.

"She's a witch," said Mama. "But they sure do have good barbecue."

Once Sidone got control of Bun's estate, she sold the pit, the motel, and the fishing camp. Then she moved to Baton Rouge and bought a white Victorian house. It was rumored that she took in boarders, all young men. She took a special fancy to a doctor's son, a troubled boy from New Orleans. In the mid-1940s, she was found murdered in her bedroom. When the police searched her closet, they discovered a hole in the wall; it connected to the closet of the doctor's son. The murder remains unsolved.

When I was a small girl, Mama decided to visit Uncle Bun's old pit. She took me and Dell along for company, with the promise of a barbecue sandwich for our trouble. The pit had changed ownership several times, but it was still the last stop before the old Swamp Road. As I stepped out of the car, I noticed a bluetick hound sleeping on the porch. From the roof, a blackened chimney emitted a stream of smoke. A hickory-scented haze hung in the air, and it smelled so luscious, I felt dizzy and hungry.

The three of us stepped inside the restaurant, the screen door creaking. "Look how it's changed," Mama said, nudging Aunt Dell.

"It's gone downhill," Dell said. "Uncle Bun had coleslaw, potato salad, French fries, and desserts." We stared at a rack of potato-chip bags, which stood next to a slot machine. If we wanted side dishes and tables with red-checkered oilcloths, then we'd come to the wrong joint. Mama said the only thing that smacked of old times was the sauce. Dell took a sneaky taste and pronounced it as Uncle Bun's.

The waitress informed us that the pit served one thing: pork sandwiches. We watched a customer open his sandwich and slather on the sauce. The meat looked to be hand shredded, slightly charred at the edges, and it gave off an irresistible aroma. Mama and Dell marched up to the counter and placed our orders. I stood on my toes and watched the cook fix our sandwiches. She was a tired-looking woman with burns up and down her forearms—grease burns, no doubt. I kept my eyes on the pork. Every strand was unique; some were long and stringy, others had crusty places, where the sauce had seared and blackened. Those were my favorite pieces.

"We're kin to this sauce," Dell told the cook.

"Sure you are," she said. "You want these sandwiches to go or eat here?"

Uncle Bun's Barbecue Sauce
Yield: About 4 cups

Part 1
1 medium onion, minced
3 tablespoons unsalted butter
2 cloves garlic, minced

Over a medium flame, sauté the onion in butter, adding the garlic when the onion starts to turn translucent. The ingredients are not rigid. Some folks start with bacon drippings rather than butter. Bun had been known to add three stalks of celery, minced, and sometimes he threw in half a green pepper, finely chopped. In some batches, he added dangerous amounts of jalapeños, and lots of garlic.

Part 2
1 cup tomato sauce
1 cup ketchup
¼ to 1 cup brown sugar

Over a low flame, stir together until sugar dissolves, then add:

1 tablespoon paprika
¼ teaspoon chili powder
1½ teaspoons dry mustard
½ teaspoon salt

2 tablespoons Worcestershire
  sauce
¼ cup cider vinegar

1½ tablespoons fresh lemon juice	1½ tablespoons powdered beef bouillon or ½ cup beef stock
1 teaspoon liquid smoke	A few grinds of fresh pepper
¼ cup water	Tabasco to taste

Over a medium-high flame, mix until smooth, using a wire whisk. Boil for five minutes. Reduce heat, then cover. Simmer one hour, stirring occasionally. Uncle Bun used to make this sauce in huge crab pots, and Mama said it kept for weeks. It is delicious brushed over ribs, chicken, and even salmon; but I have been known to eat it like soup, savoring each spoonful.

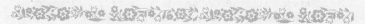

"All this time I thought the recipe was lost," Dell said as we walked back to the car.

"Bun wrote it on the wall," Mama said. "My daddy found it later."

"What makes Southern men write on the walls?" said Dell. "Remember William Faulkhurst?"

"Don't you mean Faulkner?" Mama quirked one eyebrow, as if trying to remember.

"Maybe he knew Sidone, too," Dell said.

We climbed into the car and drove off, heading south on the Swamp Road. I rode shotgun, and Dell sat in the backseat, eating one of the sandwiches. "I can understand leaving a man, or even a town," Mama was saying, "but not good barbecue."

"Forget the man. I'd rather eat pork any old day," Dell muttered, licking her fingers. Then she reached into the sack, rustling the papers, and pulled out another sandwich.

Dinner with Aunt Dell

Dell's recipes are just as weird as she is. Once she gave me a recipe for her linguine. On the index card she'd listed twelve ingredients—straightforward things like butter, Italian sausage, garlic, herbs. The instructions didn't make sense: "Cook in large skillet. Down to Mushrooms. Boil linguine in Salt for 15 to 30 minutes. Put Mushrooms in Sausage." When I questioned her, she looked exasperated and said, "It's self-explanatory." That's Dell for you. (She's never been right in the head.)

—Anonymous relative, overheard at the meat case at Piggly Wiggly, Dijon, Louisiana, 1981

One Memorial Day weekend, my husband and I drove from Tennessee to Louisiana to visit the elderly aunts. I was sitting in the backseat, watching the scenery; Mama rode shotgun, sipping Coca-Cola from a thermos. "I've made us a reservation at Motel Six," she said.

"You mean we aren't staying with the aunts?" said Will.

"I hated to burden them. They're so old and fragile," she said. "All except for Dell. We sure don't want to stay with her."

"Why not?" asked Will.

"Trust me," Mama said. We thought of Dell as an ageless Southern woman, prone to eccentricity. At bridge clubs and Christian women's events, Dell's name is whispered; and in certain circles, she is held up as an example, a cautionary tale. *Just look at Dell* ——. That's what parents in certain parts of Louisiana and Mississippi tell their children.

As soon as we checked into the motel, the clerk told us we had a message. "It's from someone called Dell," he said, squinting at a slip of paper. "She said it was important." We stepped into our room, throwing our suitcases on the bed. I fell on top of a floral luggage bag and said, "I'm starving." Two inches from my head, the phone began ringing; it had an odd trill, short and urgent, the way phones sound in foreign countries. I reached back to grab the receiver, thinking the motel clerk was calling to tell us we'd left something in the lobby. When I heard the voice, I sat up, blinking. It was Aunt Dell, inviting us over for dinner.

"I'm making my famous pot roast," she said. "You-all bring a salad."

"A salad?" I said, and the line went dead. "Wait, don't go!" I cried, but the receiver buzzed in my ear. Mama turned around and stared. "Dell's invited us for supper," I announced, then gingerly hung up the phone. "She wants us to bring—"

"I heard—a salad," said Mama, shaking her head. Her eyes flashed. "Well, I'll just step into our fully equipped kitchen and whip up something fine."

"Oh, Mama," I said, rolling my eyes. The Motel 6 didn't have a kitchen; why, it didn't even have Magic Fingers or a miniature icebox. Even if we found a supermarket with a salad bar, which was extremely unlikely in this part of Louisiana, it would not solve our dilemma. We were leery of visiting Aunt Dell. She is a voracious collector. Long ago, her dining room just disappeared. Her house is so cluttered that pathways have evolved. As you walk around, you must press your arms tightly against your sides, because you never know what will grab at you. A few years back, Dell decided to raise monkeys, but Dijon, Louisiana, is a small community, and the market soon dried up. Some people claim that Dell turned the monkeys loose in the woods, and when the moon is full, you can hear screeching.

After the monkeys, Dell decided to raise hairless cats. These vicious little creatures resemble aliens—bald and wrinkled, with huge black eyes; they are prone to lashing out from the junk heaps, clinging to your ankle with sharp claws. The last time any-one counted, which was years ago, Dell had about eighteen cats. No telling how many she had now. She claimed there was no mar-ket for them, but it didn't matter—she couldn't bear to part with a single one. Those cats were family, with names like Elvis, Jezebel, and Judas the Betrayer. My mama's elderly aunts were churchgoing women, and they were appalled by the biblical names. "Name them something else," they urged. "Name them after soap-opera stars!"

"I'm not breaking any commandments," Dell countered. "I'll name my cats anything I please." Now, sitting on the hard Motel 6 bed, Mama and I glared at each other.

"We have to go," I said. "Salad or no salad."

"I'd just as soon not," Mama said.

"I've never met Dell," said Will. His eyes glinted with mischief. He just adores to needle Mama about her relatives. "Tell me about her."

"Well," said Mama, "her blood type is sour cherry."

"Oh, don't be mean," I said.

"Blood is thicker than water," said Will.

"So is gravy," said Mama.

"Dell needs our love," I said in a preacherly tone. "Not our criticism."

"What she needs," Mama said, "is a can of Raid."

The night of the dinner, we stopped at a Pizza Hut and bought a salad to go. Then we drove in silence to my aunt's house. Dell lives out in the country, in a wooden house with an L-shaped porch. As we drove up, I stared at the cluttered yard. A long time ago, before the monkeys, she raised chickens, but they vanished one by one. Over by the pine trees, the coops were still visible. For years, guinea feathers would float by, and the monkeys would rise up on their haunches, batting the air.

Now the three of us sat in the car, gazing up at the house, afraid to move. It was wooden, painted hot pink, with lime green shutters. Dell said it was the latest style in Key West, a place she may or may not have been. With my aunt, anything was possible. Dell was affectionately known as the family "artiste." In the fifties, she colorized black-and-white photographs with a set of cheap watercolors, changing brown eyes to turquoise, blond curls to halos of flame. Everyone thought Dell's hobby was weird, but we indulged her, all the while whispering behind her back, hiding the garish, retouched photographs in deep dresser drawers. Now, when we consider Ted Turner's success with colorized black-and-white movies, we see that she was ahead of her time.

"You go first," said Will, nodding at the pine-strewn path.

"No, you," I said.

Dell's porch seemed like an obstacle course. Withered plants were piled up on the railing—geraniums, ferns, wandering Jew. It no longer resembled a porch. Scattered everywhere was a thousand years of clutter: a broken toilet; newspapers and catalogues; a battered maroon velvet chair where Dell liked to snap green beans; and an empty wire birdcage, its resident long ago devoured. In the center of the porch, she'd set up a square table, covering it with a pink tablecloth and her mother's Limoges china.

"Will you look at that," said Will, smirking. "We're dining al fresco tonight."

"Don't start," said Mama, narrowing her eyes. She put her hand on the door handle, but she didn't open it. "You don't have any room to talk. I know all about your forebears. Michael Lee told me."

"She exaggerates," he scoffed. "Anyhow, we've all got our rascals."

"Speak for yourself." Mama gave him a swift, venomous look.

"Come on, let's get out of the car," he said. "I'm hungry. I bet Dell's pot roast leaves yours in the dust."

Mama's eyes popped open wide. "What did you just say?"

"You two promised not to argue," I said.

"I lied," said Mama, balling one hand into a fist.

"Then you-all stay and fight it out. I'm going to see Dell," I said, cradling the Pizza Hut salad. I opened the door and climbed out of the backseat. Will and Mama were right behind me. Dell's house loomed in front of us.

"Let's all go at once," he said. We walked stiffly up to the house, glancing around for marauding cats. Sometimes bloody fights spring up, and the animals roll in the yard, all fur and fangs. Because they are bald, many of the toms are crisscrossed with scars. Dell claims the cats are picky about where they sleep. Over the years there have been many lovers' quarrels. I looked all around but I didn't see a single animal. Dell's front yard was empty, except for the statues, leftovers from the days when she worked at the concrete plant. She has the four seasons, assorted gargoyles, ducks, flamingos, frogs, and children. It looks like the garden of a wicked witch who could turn her victims to stone with a single glance.

We climbed the porch steps, sidestepping the clutter. Dell was nowhere in sight. Come to think of it, I hadn't seen a car in the driveway. She might not even be home; but the screen door was ajar. From somewhere deep inside, I heard yowling.

"Dell?" Mama cried. "You home?" Then, in a whisper, Mama said, "Let's hope this is her bowling night."

I peered through the torn screen mesh and saw a crooked path; it was hemmed in with Winn-Dixie bags and piles of JCPenney catalogues, then it dropped off into a sinister darkness. The interior of her house was legendary, frightening everyone from children to Electrolux salesmen. It even tried the patience of blood kin. As I opened the door and stepped inside, I set off Dell's homemade burglar-alarm system—two hundred battery-operated plastic frogs. She buys them in bulk at Wal-Mart. Marketed as motion detectors, they emit "ribbits" when the slightest thing, even sunlight, crosses their infrared "eye."

"I *thought* I heard something," Dell cried, thundering down the path, her thighs swishing together. She is a massive, pear-shaped woman, and she'd be the first to tell you about the time she went swimming—someone tried to harpoon her, she'd say, slapping her thigh. Tonight she wore a hibiscus-strewn muumuu. She was also barefoot, and her toenails were painted purple.

"Come on in," she said, her voice rising over the frantic ribbits. "Just come right on in. Supper's almost ready. Excuse the *blanking* mess."

I hadn't visited Dell in two years, not since my last trip to Louisiana, and she'd done some redecorating. The kitchen cabinets were painted wrought-iron black—"to hide grease splatters," she explained. All over the walls, she'd nailed up baskets, and plastic strings of fruit, the kind that dimestores sold in the sixties. I stared at a cat clock, its eyes and tail switching back and forth like windshield wipers. Hot peppers and herbs, all cultivated in her weedy garden, hung from wooden pegs. Two humpbacked iceboxes hummed on the canning porch. I was dying to look inside. Dell's refrigerators are perversely clean and they are always crammed full of cakes, which she freezes in bulk. She calls it her funeral food. Assorted cats snoozed on top of each icebox, a tangle of wrinkled elbows, folded hind legs, and slick skulls. Tonight they didn't resemble aliens; they looked more like Cornish hens, plucked and ready for the oven.

I looked around for a seat, but the chairs were buried under folded clothes, books of ancient green stamps, garden tomatoes, stacks of unopened mail. I set the Pizza Hut salad on a telephone book—on the cover it said, Dijon, Louisiana, 1948.

"Why, Dell," I cried, peering at the phone book. "This is an antique!"

"You can have it, honey," she said. "There's more where that came from. If antiques ever get popular, I'll be set. Why, I could be sitting on a fortune."

"Literally," Mama said, but Dell just smiled. From the living room came the sound of ribbits, and I knew the cats were stalking Will. From beneath the table, a cat slithered out, walking on tiptoe to Dell. "There you are, Eczema," she said to the animal, rubbing his bald head with her toes.

"Eczema?" Mama reached into the quagmire, digging out a purple bar stool. "You're naming your cats after skin diseases?"

"Well, he's had his problems," Dell said, facing the stove. She began rattling pot lids. Behind her, the tile counter was loaded with jars and bottles—lemon pepper, chile pepper, olive oil, Worcestershire, Tabasco, and Accent. The cabinet gaped open, revealing a jumble of other mysterious jars.

"Your roast smells good," I said.

"Aren't you sweet!" Dell picked up a wooden spoon, dipped up some gravy, and held it under my nose. "Here's you a taste," she said. "Go on; it won't bite."

It *was* good, a beefy, tomato gravy. I smacked my lips. Dell turned to my mother, offering her a sample. Mama took a delicate sip, then briefly closed her eyes. "Delicious, Dell," said Mama. "How did you make it?"

"Well, it's hard to say." Dell laughed, shrugging. She ran one hand through her cropped hair. "I just start digging in the cabinets, adding this and that. But I don't have a recipe, really. Just a method."

"What cut of meat do you use?" asked Mama.

"It depends," said Dell.

"I like a brisket," said Mama. "But it's hard to find one that's not corned."

"I use chuck roast," I said, leaning against the counter, picking up jars. Dell believed in paprika, and her tin was almost empty. A small, unlabeled mason jar caught my attention. I picked it up and shook it. The contents were the color of Atlantic Coast sand, flecked with black specks, which appeared to be cracked pepper. Dell plucked the jar from my fingers, unscrewed the lid, and poured the dark, mysterious grains into the pot. With her free hand, she picked up a spoon and stirred the particles into the gravy.

"This is my secret ingredient," Dell said, handing the jar to me. I held it up to the light. I saw red pepper flakes, sea salt, dehydrated garlic, and assorted gourmet peppers. As I gazed at the jar, some of the black flecks moved. I blinked twice, then shook my head and eyeballed the jar. Sure enough, something in the jar *was* moving. I frantically motioned for Mama.

"What?" she whispered. I held out the jar. Mama took off her glasses and squinted. Then she snatched the jar and shook it. "My stars," she said, her voice barely a whisper. "It's alive!"

"What's all this whispering?" Dell said, laying down her spoon. She glared at us. "Y'all look funny. What's the matter?"

"Dell—honey?" Mama began. "I hate to tell you, but I think your secret seasoning is ruined."

"What?" She lumbered over, her thighs swishing together. "Give it here."

"It's contaminated, Dell." Mama handed over the jar.

"Why, it's—" Dell's voice broke off. She opened the jar and stuck two fingers inside. Then she shifted her eyes at Mama. "It's just—"

"Weevils," Mama said.

"I do *not* have weevils," Dell snapped, her cheeks flushing. "These aren't nothing but doodlebugs. Little baby doodlebugs. They won't hurt a thing."

"Tell me you didn't put those things into the pot roast," Mama said, one hand rising to her mouth.

"Tons," admitted Dell. "But I'm sure the heat from the gravy killed them."

Mama and I offered to drive back to Pizza Hut, but Dell declined. "I've got an idea," she told us. She strode over to the pot, forked up the meat, and kicked a path to the sink. Two cats screeched, then shot out of a paper sack, vanishing down a forked trail.

"Elvis has left the building," Dell said, laughing.

"Who?" Mama twisted her neck.

"Elvis the cat," said Dell. "He can meow to the tune of 'Jailhouse Rock.' "

Dell stood in front of the sink, gripping the roast in one large hand, rinsing it under a stream of water. With a sigh, she set the meat down on a Limoges platter. Then she straddled a colander over a huge Pyrex bowl. Grunting, she heaved up the pot and poured in the gravy. Mama and I watched, repelled yet fascinated, as the strained "gravy" trickled into the bowl.

"That's an awful big sieve you got there," Mama said. "Big-holed. Don't you have a smaller one?"

"Oh, somewhere," said Dell.

I peered at the colander. It *was* big-holed, the perfect size for weevils to slip through. Dell cast aside the colander and reached for a glass bowl. Using a demitasse spoon, she stirred the gravy, plucking out dead doodlebugs, all the while humming "The Girl from Ipanema."

Finally it was time to eat. Dell walked around the porch, lighting candles. I tried to pull Will aside, but he was in a perverse mood. "Why are you whispering?" he said loudly, cutting his eyes at Dell. "We're all family here. Speak up or shut up."

I put my hands on my hips and said, "I guess I'll hush, then."

We sat down, shaking out our napkins. Inside the house, the frogs ribbited and the cats hissed. Mama and I took extra servings of salad.

"Why aren't you eating any roast?" said Will, looking from me to Mama.

"I'm thinking of becoming a vegetarian," said Mama.

"Me, too," I said.

"You don't know what you're missing," said Will, forking up the meat.

"Oh, yes we do," said Mama.

"Hush, now," Dell said. She lifted the delicate china gravy boat and smiled at Will. "Ready for seconds, sugar?"

Cooking
Lessons

In Miss Johnnie's Kitchen

Anybody can cook. But it takes a special person to feed the souls of her guests.

> —Miss Johnnie, sitting in a rocking chair, musing about hospitality, 1979

When I was a student nurse, I cooked for a black woman named Miss Johnnie, a cardiac patient who'd been assigned to my care. She'd suffered a mild heart attack, and the doctor had ordered a low-salt, low-cholesterol diet. After she was discharged, I made a follow-up visit at her apartment. Miss Johnnie was frail, and she had no living relatives. All of her neighbors were elderly. During the visit, she shuffled around her kitchen trying to put together a meal. I noticed how breathless she seemed; it worried me.

"Miss Johnnie," I said, "let me finish up here."

"I don't know," she said. "Cooking in a strange kitchen is like washing your hair in somebody else's bathroom."

"Well, I'm not a good cook," I confessed. "But I can learn."

"Maybe, maybe not," she said. I led her to a chair, then I pulled on an apron—she had a whole collection of them hanging on the pantry door. When supper was ready, I dished up green beans. Miss Johnnie made a face. "Honey, you're a good little nurse, but these beans are awful."

"I'm sorry," I said. "But they're healthy."

"Not if I starve, child," she said. She held up a bean. "Did you boil it in mop water?"

The next day she asked me to move her rocking chair into the kitchen, where she could monitor my activities. I was torn between wanting to please her and wanting to maintain her diet. In that sunny kitchen, with its window full of violets, we compromised. Throughout the week, she ate the prescribed food—skinless chicken breasts, a cup of boiled carrots, rice without butter. But on Friday night, I cooked with soul.

Miss Johnnie taught me that bacon drippings ruin green beans—the true secret is a scrubbed ham hock, a small chopped onion, a pinch of sugar, and a hot red-pepper pod. And all greens benefit from being nipped by Jack Frost; if your greens are store-bought, you can simulate the nipping by sticking the collards (or turnips) into the freezer for fifteen minutes or so. "Just don't forget about them," warned Miss Johnnie.

Twenty years later, my friend is gone, but her favorite dishes are celebrated every week in my kitchen. My children say, "Fix Miss Johnnie's macaroni and cheese. And her pineapple upside-down cake, too."

Every New Year's Day, I re-create her menu. I invite friends to drop by for a plate of black-eyed peas, rice, applesauce, jalapeño potatoes, collard greens, cabbage, corn bread, macaroni and cheese, oven-roasted tomatoes, and pineapple upside-down cake.

It is a meatless menu, but none of my guests seems to notice. Mama says it's due to the champagne, but I think Miss Johnnie's spirit is guiding me.

Macaroni and cheese is both soothing and filling, a hands-down favorite among children, yet it remains one of those recipes that daunts most cooks. Who has time for a cream sauce? Who wants to mess up *three* separate pans? Miss Johnnie's recipe requires two pans but no cream sauce. Once you've tasted this dish, you will never eat boxed or frozen macaroni again. Overnight, you will become a macaroni and cheese specialist. You can dress up this recipe by scattering buttered bread crumbs over the top, and you can be resourceful with cheese, tinkering with gourmet brands. It makes a fine entrée, especially when you add a mixed greens salad and yeast rolls.

Miss Johnnie's Macaroni and Cheese
Yield: 6 to 8 servings

2 cups elbow macaroni
2 tablespoons salt

Boil macaroni according to directions on the box. Meanwhile, assemble the following ingredients:

¼ cup unsalted butter, at room
   temperature
2 cups evaporated milk
   (I use Pet milk)
2 teaspoons Dijon mustard
½ teaspoon salt

½ teaspoon pepper
3 eggs, beaten
Dash Tabasco
2 pounds sharp cheddar
   cheese, grated
Paprika, for dusting

Preheat oven to 350 degrees. Drain macaroni and transfer into a big bowl. Add butter. Stir. In another bowl, pour the evaporated milk. Whisk in the Dijon mustard, salt, and pepper. Slowly add the beaten eggs and Tabasco. Using a 9 × 13-inch buttered dish (or a 2-quart casserole) spoon in the macaroni. Sprinkle with the grated cheese. Add the milk and egg mixture, lightly stirring to make sure everything is blended. Dust with paprika. Bake for approximately 50 minutes. The last ten minutes, you might have to cover it with foil. Sometimes I add a topping—½ cup bread crumbs, ¼ cup grated cheddar, and 1 tablespoon butter, cut into pieces. Mix the ingredients and add this 25 minutes before you're ready to pull the dish from the oven. As Miss Johnnie used to say, this recipe generously serves eight hungry souls or six starving ones.

When it comes to pineapple upside-down cake, I'm sure there are easier recipes, but I've never tasted one quite this delicious. Maybe it's the cast-iron pan or maybe it's the beaten egg whites. Whenever I serve this cake, there are never any leftovers. Clearly, Miss Johnnie knew her desserts.

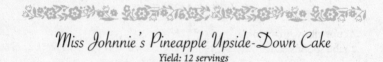

Miss Johnnie's Pineapple Upside-Down Cake
Yield: 12 servings

½ cup unsalted butter
1 cup brown sugar, packed

Preheat oven to 350 degrees. Over a low flame, melt the unsalted butter in a cast-iron skillet. Spoon in the brown sugar. Turn off the heat.

GATHER

One 20-ounce can pineapple slices   Maraschino cherries
   (drain, reserving ¼ cup juice)   Pecan halves

Arrange the pineapple slices over the brown sugar mixture. Cut left-over slices in half, and use them to line the sides of the skillet, cut sides facing in. Stick a cherry in the center of every pineapple circle. Press the pecan halves between the pineapple slices.

PREPARE

1 cup all-purpose flour	3 egg yolks (reserve whites in a
1 teaspoon baking powder	separate bowl)
½ teaspoon salt	1 cup sugar
	1 teaspoon vanilla

In a large bowl, combine the flour, baking powder, and salt, then run your hands through it. Or, if you are the finicky sort, use a sifter. Plug in an electric mixer and beat the egg yolks until they are thick. Very slowly, add the sugar. Spoon in the flour, baking powder, and salt. Add the vanilla.

Pour the mixture of egg whites into a deep bowl. Beat them with a mixer on high. When stiff peaks form, stop beating. Using a rubber spatula, fold the whites into the batter. Gently spoon the batter over the pineapple. Bake 50 minutes. Remove from the oven and invert, without cooling, onto a serving plate.

Black-Eyed Peas for New Year's
Yield: 12 generous servings

On New Year's Eve, rinse 1 cup dried black-eyed peas. Soak all night in cold water. The next morning, check your peas. Discard any "floaters." While the peas drain in a colander, fry four slices of bacon. Remove bacon; reserve for another dish—for example, bacon deviled eggs. Pour off all grease except for 2 tablespoons. Pour this grease in an 8- to 10-quart pot. Chop 1 onion, 3 stalks celery, and half a green pepper. Add these vegetables to the pot with the bacon grease and sauté over a medium flame. Mince 2 teaspoons garlic and throw in the pot. Add the peas, 1½ cups chicken stock, and 3 quarts cold water. Add 1½ pounds pigs' tails, finely chopped, or 1 smoked ham hock. Add 1 teaspoon salt, ¾ teaspoon black pepper, ⅛ teaspoon cayenne, and 1 hot red-pepper pod, whole. Bring the pot to a boil, then reduce the flame and simmer, covered, for about 1½ hours, stirring frequently. Remove the lid and cook another 30 to 45 minutes. Meanwhile, in a separate pot, cook long-grain rice, following the directions on the bag. (Orzo makes a delicious substitute.) Serve the beans over the rice.

Southern Collard Greens
Yield: 4 to 6 servings

2 teaspoons sugar	1 dried hot red-pepper pod,
Smoked ham hock	whole
3 to 4 pounds collard greens	Salt and pepper to taste

The first step is to fill a large pot with three quarts of cold water. Add the sugar and ham hock. Boil 40 minutes. If your kitchen is like Miss Johnnie's and mine, your windows will steam up. Remember that plants flourish in a kitchen where collards are cooked.

Meanwhile, wash the greens three times, changing the water each time. Lift the collards from the sink rather than letting the water drain out. After the third rinsing, if the bottom of the sink is still gritty, rinse the greens again. Pull off the stems. Then, stacking the leaves, roll them. Cut into 2-inch slices. Put collards in the pot with the ham hocks. The pot will be overflowing with greens, but don't worry—the greens will rapidly wilt. Add the hot red-pepper pod and salt and pepper to taste. Cook about 1 hour. Remove ham hock—bits of meat will fall into the greens; the more the better, but discard the fat. Serve with corn bread, which is always best baked in a cast-iron pan.

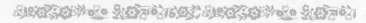

Uncork the champagne. Even though it's daylight, burn candles in every room. Rather than digging out china bowls and chafing dishes, direct your guests to the stove and let them serve themselves directly from the pots. Most people are comfortable with this arrangement; some don't like rice with their peas, and others like extra corn bread.

Raise your glass. Remember those who have blessed your life. Happy New Year, Miss Johnnie.

Fried Chicken: A Guide for the Wary

Frying a chicken separates the cooks from the dilettantes. It is messy and unhealthy, but once you master it, you can do anything. Frying chicken is harder than, say, making a soufflé. And it's a lot more painful.

—Mimi Little, frying chicken at the Home Demonstration Club, Liberty, Mississippi, 1948

At least once a month, my family begs for fried chicken. I do not like to fry chicken, or anything else involving vast quantities of oil. It can turn a clean kitchen into a battlefield—flour hanging in the air, grease splatters on the stove, and first-degree burns. Not to mention the raw chicken itself, laid out like corpses on the waxed paper. But there is something very basic, almost folksy about rolling chicken in flour and carefully dropping the pieces into sizzling oil. I myself use tongs and old, elbow-length gloves. When people call me a coward, I ignore them. I am not just serving up chicken, I tell them. I am serving up a tradition.

If this is your first time frying chicken, don't worry about side dishes. The point is to get you frying without having a conniption fit. Think of this as an experiment, an adventure in cooking. First, wear old clothes. Buy lots of paper towels and a whole, cut-up chicken. When you get home, wash the pieces in cold water and pat dry. Cut the breasts in half. Place the chicken in a huge bowl and cover with buttermilk. Cover the bowl with plastic wrap and set in the refrigerator. Marinate all day, or overnight. Be sure to let the pieces soak for at least 1 hour at room temperature before proceeding to the next step: Ice-cold chicken seems to repel flour.

When you are ready to cook, drain the chicken. In another bowl, add 1 cup all-purpose flour, 1 teaspoon kosher salt, and a few grinds of pepper. If desired, throw in 1 or 2 tablespoons paprika and a pinch of cayenne. Using *one* hand only (keep the other free to turn on the faucet), dip the chicken into the flour. Really pat it on. Some cooks like to fry chicken while listening to Verdi—*La Forza del Destino*—but Bruce Springsteen will work, too. After a while, the seasoned flour gets lumpy, but that's okay. Just add more flour. Set the pieces on a large platter. Some cooks let the chicken "rest," then they re-flour. (Oh, go on and use both hands. You can clean up later.)

Pour an inch or two of vegetable oil into a heavy skillet. A cast-iron one is traditional, but any deep skillet will work. When the oil reaches 350 degrees—in other words, when you drop in a piece of bread and it sizzles—slowly add your chicken. Cook ten minutes per side for breasts and eight minutes for smaller pieces. Resist the urge to keep turning the chicken because this tends to loosen the crust.

Just because the chicken is browning does not mean it's done. I know a woman who decided to give a platter of fried chicken to an ailing neighbor. The pal fried two chickens, saving some for her own family. After she ran next door with the platter, she patted herself on the back, thinking she'd done a good deed *and* managed to feed her sons. But when she stepped into her own kitchen, her boys held up raw drumsticks. The woman called the neighbor and said, "You might want to stick that chicken in the oven."

There's a remedy for undercooked chicken. When the meat starts to brown, some people lower the flame and put on a lid, steeping the chicken for about 30 minutes. This is controversial among chicken fryers. My aunt Minnie always used a tightly fitting lid; her chicken was never pimiento red at the bone and the meat was moist and tender. If you choose this method, remember to remove the lid toward the end of your frying time; turn up the heat, and cook the chicken ten more minutes. This will make it crispy. My mama and grandmama never used a lid. They browned the chicken on all sides on medium-high heat, then they turned the burner to medium low and cooked the chicken for thirty minutes, turning each piece periodically. This is the fried chicken of my childhood; I used to wrap it in a napkin and stuff it into my lunch box.

When it comes to frying chicken, it's important to find your own style—part of the fun is experimenting, but the best part is eating. Roll up your sleeves and dig in. And don't forget to save the wishbone.

Shrimp 101

Buying seafood is a lot like picking up a woman at a bar—you got to smell them before taking them home.

—Anonymous patron, drinking beer at Florabama, located on the Florida-Alabama state line, November 1992

Ten years ago, I ordered boiled shrimp at a local fast-food eatery and was stricken with shellfish poisoning. As the family always says, leave it to me to order the most dangerous thing on a menu. Because of the sickness, I grew wary of cooking shrimp at home. For years I cruised past the iced-down seafood at Kroger. Sometimes the smell was a little strong, and I'd push my cart while holding my nose, a trick that requires skill, especially if you have a cart that wobbles.

The next time you happen to go swimming in the Gulf of Mexico, cup some water in your hands. This is how fresh shrimp ought to smell. Now when I approach the seafood section at Kroger, the clerks shy away. "Here comes the sniffer," they say, reaching into the glass case, bringing up a sample. "This is against the law," they tell me, but they drag out the shrimp anyway.

I grew up in Louisiana, and I have a vivid memory of driving to Cypremort Point for boiled crabs. Fresh shrimp was something I took for granted, like air. After we moved to Tennessee, my mother bought frozen seafood from the Piggly Wiggly. As she tore off the paper and stared down at the block of ice, with bits of gray shrimp poking out, it broke her heart. "The poor little things," she'd say. "They look like snails in a glacier."

Since then, landlocked groceries have come a long way. In our local stores you can buy lobster, prawns, clams, salmon, and five kinds of shrimp. As a rule, I don't buy tiger shrimp—it's cheap but tough. I opt for previously frozen medium shrimp, sometimes large if it's on sale.

There are many varieties of shrimp. The most common is the Gulf of Mexico brown. The least flavorful, these shrimps can be recognized in the seafood case by their brownish gray shells. If you like a mild nutty flavor, try the Gulf white shrimp. I prefer Gulf of Mexico pinks, pulled from the waters of the Carolinas and Florida. They are pink or pale orange. My father loved Royal Red shrimp, which are delectable yet costly. He called them "ruby reds" in honor of their color. These shrimp are found in deep waters off the continental shelf, as well as the Gulf and the South Atlantic. Whatever type of shrimp you buy—follow this simple method:

Foolproof Recipe for Boiled Shrimp
Serves 2 to 6, depending on appetites

WHAT YOU NEED

Two 12-ounce cans of beer
3 to 6 cups cold water
Kosher salt
3 lemons, quartered and
   slightly squeezed into the
   cold water
8 dashes Tabasco (or more)

1 packet shrimp boil*
Whole peppercorns, as desired
   (I use 1 teaspoon)
1 onion, quartered
1 bay leaf
Newspaper
2 pounds shrimp**

*Seafood boil comes in jars or dry packets. The liquid boil is potent: a little goes a long way. Advanced cooks seem to prefer the liquid over the milder packets. It's also fun to make your own boil. Study the ingredients on the box, gather your own supplies, and experiment.

**In my family this feeds exactly three people—adjust your amount accordingly.

PROCEDURE

Pour beer and water into a large pot. Add a couple of handfuls of kosher salt; cup your hand and pour a mound in the center. Repeat three times. Shrimp require salt—don't be cowardly. Add lemons, Tabasco, shrimp boil, peppercorns, onion, and more beer, if you've got any left over. My husband adds sugar (in addition to the salt) because he saw it on a cooking show. Mama said he'd be a fool to do it, but his shrimp are delectable. He adds a scant ¼ cup granulated sugar to a huge vat of water. (He cooks the shrimp outside, in a giant pot, on a gas burner. On this same contraption, he boils lobsters in lemon water, spiked with vodka, claiming it's the only humane method.)

While you wait for the water to boil, spread the newspaper over the table. Add a pile of paper napkins. Iced tea is a nice touch. When the water reaches a rolling boil, add the shrimp. Bring the water to a second boil. Cook 3 to 4 minutes. Keep an eye on the clock. DO NOT OVER-COOK. You'll be sorry if you do. The shrimp will be so tough you can use them to break windows. Some people boil small red potatoes and corn on the cob in the shrimp water—this makes a one-pot feast.

Now remove the pot from the heat. Cover the pot and let the shrimp steep 5 minutes. Drain. Peel and eat. Pass cocktail sauce, sliced lemon, and saltine crackers. Purists eschew the crackers, but I myself like to build little sandwiches. First, take a saltine, add a shrimp, and drizzle with cocktail sauce. The best sauce, by the way, is homemade; it takes less than two minutes to make, but I've seen my brother make it in thirty seconds flat. Just mix 1 cup ketchup, the juice of one lemon, a little minced garlic, a dash of Tabasco, and ½ teaspoon horseradish—or more. You can tinker with this—it's not a recipe, just a procedure. If you are serving potatoes and corn, pass the butter.

This meal cries out for a screened-in porch and lots of candles. Eat barefoot and play old blues records. Use an old metal bucket for the shells. For the fussy, set out finger bowls and lots of paper towels. Key Lime Pie is a nice complement, but watermelon is traditional. Slice it open on the table, spitting the seeds onto the newspaper. When you are finished, roll up the newspaper with the shells and seeds and corncobs. Your dishes are done. Now, walk out into the grass, stirring up the lightning bugs. Turn on the hose and wash up. Then collapse in the hammock.

꿍 ꃄ

After you have mastered the art of boiled shrimp, you are ready for two upscale recipes, shrimp Alfredo and shrimp *étouffée*. Both recipes are delicious and rich, not something you'd want to serve every day. But if you love shrimp and need a party dish, one that offers a taste of Louisiana, then you can't go wrong with these dishes.

Mama's Shrimp Alfredo

Yield: 4 to 6 servings

1 stick butter
¾ cup chopped green onions
2 medium onions, chopped
½ green bell pepper, chopped
1 envelope Knorr Alfredo mix

1 small can Pet evaporated
  milk
1 to 1½ pounds raw shrimp,
  peeled, deveined, and split
  along the tail

In a large pan, melt the butter. Sauté the onions and bell pepper. Add the Alfredo mix and Pet milk. Stir. Add the shrimp. Cook about 5 minutes. Serve over fettucini.

No one likes to prepare a meal that requires all-day cooking. These two shrimp dishes are time-efficient; you'll have time to visit with your company. Mama keeps a bag of Key West shrimp in her freezer, in case unexpected guests appear at supper time. Then she can decide which recipe to prepare. Mama says they are both "company acceptable."

Mama's Louisiana Étouffée

Yield: 4 to 6 generous servings

3 green onions, chopped
2 medium onions, chopped
½ green bell pepper, chopped
½ red bell pepper, chopped
2 stalks celery, chopped fine
1 stick unsalted butter
1 tablespoon all-purpose flour

1 to 1½ pounds raw shrimp,
  split
1 bay leaf
Salt and pepper to taste
Juice of 1 lemon, plus 1
  teaspoon zest

Sauté the onions, peppers, and celery in the butter. Cook until the onions are crystal clear. Add the flour, stirring until dissolved. Add the shrimp along with the bay leaf, salt, and pepper. Cook 7 minutes. Squeeze one lemon over the *étouffée*. Add a little zest. Remove bay leaf before serving. If you want to impress your impromptu guests, add long-grain rice, a green salad with tangerine slices (and a sesame-orange vinaigrette), and garlic bread. A store-bought cheesecake is a welcome touch. Remember to light candles. Find a jazz station on the radio. Briefly close your eyes and give thanks—sitting down to a table with good food and good friends is one of life's grandest pleasures.

Cooking Lessons

Potato Salad

Potato salad is our friend. It will never let you down. It's a shame we have to eat it, but that's life.

> —Mabel Wauford, spinster and home economics teacher, 1969

When we lived in New Orleans, my mama gave loud dinner parties. I remember hiding behind the wrought-iron banister, waiting for her to carry in the tray of flambéed ducks. (Her secret was to soak a box of sugar cubes in rum, and then arrange the unlit cubes around the duck. A match sent everything up in flames.) She can even turn canned soup into an event, garnishing it with homemade croutons or thin slices of lemon. And her potato salad is renowned—dusted with paprika, then decorated with bell pepper rings, it was frequently greeted with applause.

Just don't ask her for a recipe. She likes to be the family's sole source of perfect food. Mama doesn't like rivals in the kitchen. She says this is because she went to a girls' school in New Orleans, and it warped her. Her motto is: Never share men or recipes because something is bound to get stolen.

A few years ago, at a family potluck, Mama asked me to bring potato salad. Assuming I would buy something at the deli, Mama thoughtfully provided her red-potato salad. She was speechless when I showed up with a bowl of whipped salad, from one of my grandmother's old recipes—it looks like cold, lumpy mashed potatoes, but it's glorious. As I uncovered the bowl and set it on the table, my brother said, "Cool! Mimi's salad!"

By the end of the meal, my bowl was empty, with just a few skid marks. Mama's salad had one scoop missing. "I don't know what the world is coming to," she said, peering into her bowl. "There's mashed-potato salad and fried-potato salad, and even crab and potato salad." She sighed. "I was reading a magazine at the beauty shop, and I saw a recipe for Potato Salad *Olé*. It had black beans and jalapeños in it."

"I know someone who puts sun-dried tomatoes in her salad," I said. "It's good, too."

"I wouldn't eat it." She drew her lips into a thin line. "Why not take potato salad to another level? Add asparagus—"

"I have," I said. "It was delicious."

". . . or strawberries," she said. "Why not substitute Cool Whip for the mayonnaise?"

My brother walked into the kitchen. "Sis? That was the best salad. Can you get me the recipe?"

"I've never seen you eat so much," Mama said to Jimmy, her voice cracking.

"But it's good," he said.

"I always hated cold mashed potatoes." Mama tore off a sheet of Saran Wrap and pressed it over her salad. "That's why I don't have the recipe."

"Well, I do," I said.

"I could probably make it again," Mama said, scooting her left-over salad into the refrigerator. "I've seen your grandmother make it a thousand times. But go ahead and write it down. And don't leave out a single thing."

Mimi's Mashed-Potato Salad
Yield: 6 to 8 servings

Boil 7 large potatoes, preferably russet, in sugar-and-salt water (4 tablespoons sugar and 3 tablespoons salt added to 1 large pot of water). When the potatoes are soft, drain, peel, and cut into chunks. Mix 2 tablespoons bacon drippings (or 2 tablespoons extra-virgin olive oil) with 1½ tablespoons white vinegar (Mimi used plain old white vinegar, but a good brand of white wine or champagne vinegar would be a nice touch). Pour over the potatoes. Let the potatoes sit for 30 minutes. Meanwhile, assemble the following ingredients:

6 hard-boiled eggs, grated (or finely chopped)	¾ cup homemade mayonnaise, or Hellmann's
½ cup sweet pickles with 1 or 2 tablespoons of their juice	½ cup sour cream
3 stalks celery, finely chopped	Salt and pepper to taste
1 medium onion, finely chopped	Paprika (optional)
1 small jar chopped pimientos, drained	1 tomato, sliced (optional)
	1 green bell pepper, sliced into rings (optional)

Roughly mash the potatoes, then add the eggs, pickles, celery, onion, pimientos, mayonnaise, and sour cream. Salt and pepper to taste. If desired, sprinkle with paprika. Serve on lettuce leaves, and garnish with tomato wedges and green bell pepper rings.

This salad is good hot or cold, but the flavor peaks after 24 hours. It's even good if you don't mash the potatoes, and it lends itself to all sorts of variations. Depending on my mood, and the contents of my refrigerator, I've been known to add 1 chopped bell pepper, a sprinkling of fresh dill, an extra jolt of vinegar, or a generous teaspoon of dry English mustard.

Sometimes, though, the heart cries out for a spirited salad, one without a drop of mayonnaise. My daddy's potato salad recipe was refreshing on scalding-hot summer days; and it was exemplary at picnics, as you never had to worry about the mayonnaise turning.

Ralph's Bayou Potato Salad
Yield: 6 to 8 servings

2½ pounds red Irish potatoes
3 eggs
1 packet shrimp or crab boil
  (optional)
5 cloves garlic, pressed
½ cup vinegar*

1½ teaspoons Dijon mustard
⅓ cup extra-virgin olive oil
½ cup finely chopped onion
3 slices bacon, fried and
  crumbled (optional)
Fresh parsley

My father used whatever was in the pantry; white wine vinegar works well, but feel free to experiment. I've used tarragon, dill, and garlic-rosemary.

Boil the potatoes and eggs. If you want to add punch to your salad, add one packet of shrimp boil to your water. My daddy boiled his eggs and potatoes in the same pan. In a smallish bowl, whisk together the garlic, vinegar, mustard, and olive oil.

When the potatoes are tender, drain. Do not peel, unless you are finicky about these things. Cut the potatoes into rough cubes or slices. Peel and chop the eggs. In a large bowl, mix together the potatoes, eggs, and chopped onion. Add the vinaigrette. Let this salad sit at room temperature for 3 hours before serving so the potatoes can absorb the dressing. Garnish with crumbled bacon and parsley.

Cooking Lessons

My mother did not approve of this salad. She believed in mayonnaise, celery, peppers, and pickle relish. She always promised to give me her recipe, but she'd get tongue-tied and leave out essential ingredients. Until Mama divulges her recipe, I will keep experimenting.

After years of chopping vegetables and pickles, I discovered a potato salad that's quick and delicious. It has a tangy mayonnaise sauce and involves a minimum of chopping—it's perfect for the harassed cook. I first made it on an afternoon when I was pressed for time: Eight people were coming for dinner. I wasn't sure how it would be received, but everyone loved it. Except Mother, of course.

"My salad is ten times better than this," she said.

"Just taste it," I said, passing her the bowl. "It's not fair to condemn a salad you've never tried."

"Oh, all right," she said. She spooned up a little serving. Then she took a tiny bite, chewing thoughtfully.

"Well?" I said, leaning across the table. "Isn't it fabulous?"

"Pretty good," she admitted. "But I've had better."

Easy Potato Salad for Exhausted Cooks
Yield: 8 servings

Fill a large pan with cold water; add 2 tablespoons salt and 2 tablespoons sugar. Add 8 to 10 small red potatoes and bring to a boil over a medium flame. Don't bother to peel the potatoes, unless potato skin repels you. When the potatoes are knife-tender, drain into a colander. Meanwhile, chop 4 to 6 green onions, tops and bottoms—more, if you like your salad oniony. Now chop approximately ¼ cup of fresh parsley. When the potatoes are cool enough to handle, quarter and put in a large bowl. Add the parsley and onions. Sprinkle with kosher salt, celery salt, paprika, a pinch of sugar, and a few grinds of pepper.

Now, find a small bowl and assemble the following ingredients—you can be a little sloppy, adjusting the flavor to taste. Add:

3 tablespoons mayonnaise (sometimes I use 2 tablespoons mayonnaise and 1 tablespoon sour cream)
1 tablespoon honey mustard
1 tablespoon honey
Juice of ½ lemon (sometimes I use lime)
Few dashes Tabasco

A jolt of vinegar (about ¼ teaspoon—I prefer champagne or white wine vinegar)
Another pinch of sugar
Paprika, salt, and pepper to taste (I like lots of pepper and paprika)
1 sweet red pepper, sliced into rings (optional)

Whisk and pour over the potatoes. Gently blend, mixing the sauce in. The flavor of this salad improves by the hour. Garnish with a few red bell pepper rings if desired.

Potato salad goes with anything. Its simplicity is matched by its versatility. You can gussy it up with lettuce leaves, serve it in hollowed-out green peppers, or heap it on paper plates. You can serve it roasted, dilled, creamy, chunky; you can throw in gourmet mustard, blend a little sour cream into the mayonnaise, or squirt in ketchup. Crisp, crumbled bacon lifts any potato salad into high, if unhealthy, art. It's also good with pimiento-stuffed olives, chopped or sliced.

Whenever you prepare potato salad, remember that it is an ancient cure for impotency. It was precious in medieval Europe, selling for nearly a thousand dollars a pound. The libidinous effect is apparently heightened by adding onions, parsley, chives, or dill. Dish up a generous portion to your beloved. If he asks what you're up to, do not elaborate. Do not explain. Smile when he takes a second helping.

Making Corn Bread

If you don't know how to make corn bread, then you are missing out on one of the joys of life.

—Miss Johnnie, soul cook and philosopher

Of all the basic recipes the novice must attempt, corn bread tops the list. Whenever I serve it at casual dinner parties, it's always a hit. Even native Southerners express delight and awe, digging in for seconds and thirds. "You *made* this?" they'll ask.

Yes, and I'm almost embarrassed to admit how foolproof it is. It's down-home and filling. Furthermore, it's adaptable. You can add jalapeños and corn for a Southwestern flair. Some people throw in grated cheese, and I've even seen a recipe that called for pecans. The latest corn bread fashion statement is to pour the batter into cute cast-iron molds—flowers or long, curved chile peppers lend a whimsical touch to any meal.

To make traditional Southern corn bread, pour 2 teaspoons of bacon drippings into the bottom of an 8-inch square pan (or a well-seasoned cast-iron skillet). Pam or vegetable oil will work if you are worried about cholesterol. Heat the pan in a 400-degree oven. Watch it very carefully, because oil is volatile, and if it burns, or even comes close to burning, you'll have to throw out the drippings and start over. Or not. Some people never grease their cast-iron skillets—they just stick the pan into a hot oven and let it sit there for about three or four minutes. Then they remove the skillet and immediately add the cornmeal mixture. This requires a highly seasoned skillet, one that is totally black. In the old days, they were saturated with lard and placed into a wood-burning fire.

No one approves of drippings anymore. Fearful of the heart and arteries, today's cooks rely on Pam. But it's an undeniable fact: Bacon grease adds a certain depth to the batter, even though it saturates the bloodstream. My mother, the cholesterol expert, says Wesson oil makes an agreeable substitute, but she personally doesn't know anyone who uses a vegetable-oil spray. "If you are going to do that," she says, "then why bother making corn bread?"

Remove the pan from the oven. Tilt the pan slightly, making sure that every bit of the surface is covered with a thin coating of grease. Now you're ready to add the batter—which you have made, of course, while the pan was heating.

When it comes to making a batter, you need to be informed about cornmeal. There are two types, white and yellow. Whichever you choose is more telling about your family heritage than a file from the DAR. The color of the meal means life and death to a Southerner—in fact, you might say it's a culinary Mason-Dixon line. Yankees seem to prefer yellow meal with sugar, which makes a sweeter, cakier type of bread; but if you ask any Southerner which type of cornmeal he prefers, white wins hands down. Many Southerners believe that white corn, specifically Silver Queen, is the nectar of the vegetable garden. Yellow corn is what you feed to the cows and pigs, not humans.

Since corn bread is only as good as its meal, you'll want to use an exceptional brand. There are whole grain and stone-ground meals, not to mention self-rising. With the exception of Jiffy-Mix, which is one of my mother's deep, dark, culinary secrets, my motto is no self-rising. I prefer Hodgson Mill, a whole grain, stone-ground meal that's made in Teutopolis, Illinois. It comes in both white and yellow. Finding your favorite brand takes time—and a lot of corn bread. If you aren't pleased with the offerings at your local grocery, it might be worth the trouble to cultivate a Southern friend so he or she can mail you stone-ground white meal (as the friendship deepens, you can request pecans, cane syrup, and slow-cooking grits. Fact: Southerners just love to share food).

Now, back to the batter. Measure out:

¾ cup cornmeal	1 egg, beaten
1 cup all-purpose flour	1 cup milk or buttermilk
2 teaspoons to ¼ cup sugar	1 teaspoon salt
(optional)	3 teaspoons baking powder

Mix it all up and pour into the pan. Bake 25 minutes at 400 degrees. Cool. Cut into squares, slice open, and butter. The sugar is entirely optional. Many Southerners hate sugar in their corn bread. I myself like Yankee corn bread, the sweeter the better, except when I'm using it for stuffing. Buttermilk, as opposed to sweet milk (note to beginning cooks: this does not mean condensed milk, or milk with sugar—it's plain old cow's milk) makes a moister product. My grandmother swore by it, claiming it put a bit of magic in corn bread (it did the same thing for her biscuits).

So there you have it—a corn bread recipe that you can make in less than thirty minutes. There's no yeast to proof, no bread to rise and knock down. And if you are feeling adventurous, the variations are endless. If you want to be truly decadent, add 1 cup sour cream to any corn bread recipe—it turns corn bread into velvet.

After you've made a few batches of corn bread, you'll be ready to branch out. Recipes for hoecakes, johnnycakes, hush puppies, and jalapeño bread can be found in nearly every cookbook. Some "recipes" go back generations, like the invalid's mush in *Dishes*

and Beverages of the Old South by Martha McCulloch-Williams (Knoxville: University of Tennessee Press, 1988), or the firm johnnycake that was supposed to "journey" well. Me, I'd really like to see hoecakes cooked on an actual hoe. This seems like a cross between gardening and cooking—the ultimate activity for any true Southerner.

I rarely have any leftover cornbread, but I've been told it freezes well. It's also the perfect accompaniment to white beans, barbecue, chili, and fried catfish. My grandmother used to make Louisiana Couche-Couche, a concoction that caused me and my baby brother to sit up and beg like puppies.

Mimi's Louisiana Couche-Couche
Yield: Will feed one adult and two children

Into a large bowl, mix 2 cups cornmeal, 1½ teaspoons salt, and 1 teaspoon baking powder. Add 1½ cups milk and stir. The batter will appear somewhat mushy—this is normal. Heat 1½ cup oil in a heavy skillet. Add the cornmeal mixture to the oil. Over a medium flame, let the batter form a crust—this takes about 5 minutes. Stir, then reduce the flame. Cover the pan and cook 15 minutes. Serve with milk (for a cereal) or douse it with cane syrup. This is a soothing dish for children who are recovering from an appendectomy or tonsillectomy.

When it comes to leftovers in my house, there's only one answer: corn bread and milk. Crumble a chunk or two into a tall glass, adding cold milk. Using an iced-tea spoon, mush it all up. Eat very slowly, savoring each bite, with your feet propped up on a stool. This is the ultimate comfort food—the sole reason corn bread was invented.

Cooking Lessons

How to Make a Coconut Cake

Nobody gets into heaven until they've made a coconut layer cake.

—Aunt Tempe, reminiscing about baking on various deathbeds: 1968, 1972, 1988, 1990, 1997

"A coconut cake," says my friend Margaret Jane, her voice barely above a whisper, "is a thing of beauty." She once described a cake that was brought to a family funeral—how it sat on the mahogany sideboard, ruling over the chess pies and checkerboard cakes. "That cake," Margaret Jane said, "set the tone for my life."

In the South, coconut cakes are legendary, possessing equal amounts of fluff and mystery. At parties you will find one surrounded by women, all of them begging for the recipe; but it's the culinary equivalent of the Hope diamond. You admire it, you crave it, but it's out of your reach.

Aunt Tempe baked cakes for a living in a small Louisiana town. The coconut layer was her specialty. When anyone asked for her recipe, she pretended not to hear. She'd pat her hearing aid and say: "Sorry. My battery is on the blink." As a rule, she did not divulge any recipes. Her livelihood demanded that the locals remain ignorant. If they started making their own cakes, not to mention chicken-and-broccoli casseroles, then Tempe would have to find a new career. When family (and her dearest friends) asked for a recipe, Tempe would soften. She'd throw out tidbits, but never quite a whole recipe. Like all of the aunts, Tempe was masterful at changing the subject, or backtracking. She'd start to list the ingredients, and then she'd remember a story about a man who killed his girlfriend. "Fed her a poisoned sour-cream sandwich," she would say, her eyes wide. "It was a short, but painful, death." Then she'd tell you about a man who shot his mistress over flour. The man had preferred self-rising, but the woman clung to all-purpose.

These stories only fueled our curiosity. We always tried to veer the conversation back to cake baking. "How many cups of flour does it take?" we'd say. "For what?" Tempe would ask, her eyes blinking open wide.

"For your coconut cake," we'd say.

"Oh, that." She'd wave her hand. "It takes eight days to make that cake. And that's the easy part."

I can't remember a Christmas or a wedding, not to mention Sunday dinner, without one of Tempe's cakes; she excelled in baking checkerboards along with cakes shaped like leaves, baseball diamonds, and swimming pools. Once she made a planet earth cake, complete with oceans and continents. But the coconut layer was my favorite. It took its place of honor on my great-grandmother's glass pedestal—three layers of glistening icing, with a dusting of fresh coconut, garnished with sugared fruit.

Ten years ago, Aunt Tempe was rushed to the hospital with chest pains. The doctors feared she'd suffered a heart attack. The three daughters—Dell, Lula, and Gracie—gathered around her hospital bed, watching their mama breathe through an oxygen mask. "I see a tunnel," Tempe said, holding up one withered hand. "Why, there's Mama! And her mama!"

With a little jerk, Tempe's head fell to her chin. She exhaled, a tremor ran through her body, and then she was still.

"She's gone," said Gracie, closing her mama's eyes.

"And she's taken her recipes to the grave," said Dell.

Between Gracie's fingers, one of Tempe's eyes cracked open. "I heard that," she said, pinching Dell's chubby arm. "I was just kidding. I ain't ready to die."

"Just in case," said Dell, "tell us how you make those coconut cakes. Is it true that you beat six egg whites with a teaspoon of salt and then fold them into the whipped cream?"

"I'll tell you my secret," Tempe said, beckoning them with a crooked finger. "I use a mix."

"No!" the girls cried.

"It's the truth." She nodded, smiling. "Duncan Hines White Supreme. And canned coconut milk. But if you grate a little fresh coconut over the finished cake, you can fool the experts. Use a carrot peeler for the coconut. It works like a charm."

A nurse was standing in the door. "Great news!" she said, beaming at Tempe. "We're letting you go home."

"What about my heart attack?" Tempe asked.

"You didn't have one," said the nurse. "It was an upper gastric attack."

"What the *blank* is that?" asked Dell, looking horrified.

"Gas," said the nurse.

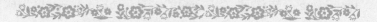

Tempe's Blue-Ribbon Coconut Cake
Yield: 12 to 14 servings

Note: This cake requires eight days before you can serve it—three to make it and five to wait.

DAY 1

Make the Filling

1½ cups fresh or frozen
    coconut, grated
One 16-ounce carton sour
    cream

1½ cups confectioners' sugar
1 teaspoon vanilla

Blend all the ingredients. Cover and refrigerate 24 hours.

DAY 2

Make the Cake

Make 1 Duncan Hines white cake, following the directions on the box. Bake in two greased and floured 9-inch pans. Cool layers on a rack.

½ cup coconut milk (fresh,
    frozen, or canned)
¼ cup white sugar

½ teaspoon vanilla

Make the Glaze

Combine the coconut milk and sugar in a saucepan. Over medium-high flame, stir constantly until the sugar melts. Add vanilla.

Glaze the Cake

Using a length of thread, split each layer in half. Handle gently—layers are fragile. Using a toothpick, poke holes in all four layers. Using a pastry brush, paint the layers with the glaze. Let sit 5 minutes. Repeat until glaze is gone. Let layers sit 24 hours, covered and refrigerated, before frosting.

Fill and Assemble the Cake

Set one layer split side up and spread with the filling. Sprinkle with ½ cup coconut. Repeat with the remaining layers. Let sit for 30 minutes after assembling the layers.

Make the Frosting

1 large carton heavy whipping cream	⅛ teaspoon cream of tartar
¾ cup granulated sugar	Fresh or frozen coconut, grated, for garnish

Pour the cream into the bowl of your mixer, and beat gently until it thickens. Switch to high speed, beating the cream until peaks form. Add the sugar and cream of tartar. Beat another minute. Frost the sides and top of cake. Garnish with coconut. Be forewarned: Avalanches do occur. Some people find it necessary to secure the layers with toothpicks.

If you're short of time, or your mixer is broken, frost the cake with one 8-ounce carton of Cool Whip mixed with 1 cup sour cream and sugar to taste. Candied violets are a nice complement; serve with vanilla coffee made from freshly ground beans.

WAITING

Clear out a space in the refrigerator, adjusting the shelves if necessary. Cover the cake—a large glass dome is best—and refrigerate for five days. Serves 12 to 14. Or, as Aunt Tempe used to say, one half for me, and one half for you.

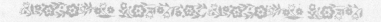

Sourdough Starter Mystique

Good bread, like good loving, can't be rushed.

—Anonymous baker, Dijon, Louisiana, 1998

All summer, my mother's friend Geraldine has been experimenting with sourdough starter. Her kitchen counters are lined with jars, each one topped with a square of cheesecloth. "So the starter can breathe," she explains to me and Mama. Geraldine can't get a single batch to bubble, but that doesn't stop her. She makes a fresh starter every day, so by the end of the week, her countertops are loaded with jars, all in various stages of souring. On the side of each jar, she writes the date. In seven days, the failed experiments get poured down the sink.

Geraldine's kitchen smells pleasantly yeasty, as if the room has witnessed years of intense baking. Some of the jars resemble buttermilk, and others look like watered-down paste. In some cases, the liquid has separated, with three inches of cloudy scum floating on top. When this happens, Geraldine whips out a wooden spoon and stirs the starter, carefully replacing the cheesecloth lid with a rubber band.

"What am I doing wrong?" she asks, but I don't know. I myself have failed to make a starter bubble. Mama stands off to the side in a patch of sunlight, holding up a jar. She has always had a mystical touch in the kitchen. In her presence, biscuits fluff up, roux thicken, and pie crusts rise to the ceiling. Whenever she wants to make a pie, all she has to do is reach up and grab a tin. And if you ask for her technique, she pretends she's just lucky, an intuitive cook.

We sit down at Geraldine's long oak table, sipping ginger tea and studying the starter recipes. She uses 3 tablespoons sugar, 1 cup of water (100 degrees), 1 package instant dry yeast, ¼ teaspoon dry ginger, and 1 cup all-purpose flour. Geraldine is a native Southerner, but she married a man from California who had a taste for sourdough bread. The husband died, but Geraldine's mission continued.

In all of the cookbooks, the ingredients called for the same ingredients: yeast, lukewarm water, sugar, and all-purpose flour. One recipe was yeastless, relying on wild, airborne spores. "I think you have to live in California for that," Mama says. Geraldine and I nod.

"Have you tried a pinch of ginger?" asks Mama.

"Many times," says Geraldine.

"And you keep it warm?"

"Eighty degrees on the dot," says Geraldine. She sighs. "The only time my starter bubbles is the first day, when I add the yeast and everything else. It's downhill after that."

"I love baking bread." Mama sighs. "The way it rises and falls. Just like a man. Lord, it teaches me to be patient."

"Some men could use a little extra yeast." Geraldine smiles.

"That's why Viagra was invented," says Mama, laughing. "Yeast for the libido."

When it's time to leave, Geraldine hands out jars of the experimental starter. "Here, you girls try," she says. "I made them fresh this morning."

I drive home, set my jar on the counter, and begin a diary. The entries are always the same: Stirred once. No bubbles. At the end of seven days, I pour my batch down the sink. Then I call Mama. "It's bubbling," she says.

"We'd better call Geraldine," I say.

"Already have," Mama says. "She's on her way over. We're going to make bread."

"I don't get it." I shake my head. "How come yours bubbled and nobody else's will?"

"I don't know what I did," Mama says, laughing. "Food just likes me. And I like it."

One-Pot Meals

A one-pot meal, combining the entrée and sides, can be a working cook's best friend. While they are not technically considered sides, many cooks rely on pinto beans, chicken and dumplings, chicken soup, and chili. Corned beef, carrots, and potatoes can be cooked in a single pot, too; yet when dished up on the plate, each food holds its own. Served on a rainy spring night, when the air still holds a wintery snap, any one-pot dish is consoling—and is usually greeted with whoops and shouts.

—From a recipe by Cousin Hettie Lynn Minx, composed in
her kitchen, Liberty, Mississippi, 1989

The speed of family life can wear down the most energetic home cook. Your heart may cry out for leg of lamb or chateaubriand, but there is simply no time for such frills. In a house with children, meals are not planned in solitude, with the quiet wisping around you like organdy curtains. Curling up with a cookbook seems like a distant dream. Just as you are searing the chicken breasts, a small voice calls out, "Mom, we're late for basketball practice!"

If it's not basketball, it's soccer practice, junior high football games, teacher conferences, music lessons, trips to the dermatologist and orthodontist. And through it all, children must be fed at regular intervals—around food fetishes and the pickiest of palates. My oldest son won't eat cheese, and the baby loves cheese but won't touch anything with nuts, bread crumbs, mayonnaise, mustard, ketchup, or sautéed onions. Add to this a husband who despises casseroles, spicy foods, and pasta, and you've got a frustrated cook.

When you work at home, people believe you have time to squander. They picture you lolling about on a silk chaise, talking on the phone, watching *All My Children*. You supposedly have all day to cook: a pot of beef stroganoff simmering on the burner and a loaf of bread rising in the pantry. People don't understand why, at the end of the day, you are rushing around in sweatpants, trying to defrost a block of frozen chili in the microwave. "Not this again!" they cry.

"I've been working," you'll say.

"You've been *home* all day!" they cry.

I myself always had an image of George Sand dining on tea and scones, with maybe an occasional piece of shortbread, but you know she had to eat something more substantial.

Even if you live alone, without so much as a goldfish, the subject of food will eventually surface. One meal a day, seven days a week, adds up to 365 meals a year. This can be taxing—the building of menus, the shopping for ingredients, the actual preparation and cleanup. And this is only one meal a day! The pressure can mount. Twenty-four hours later the body cries out again for sustenance, and the whole cycle starts over. Even if you don't cook, the soul tires of fast food—or as my cousin Jeannie calls it, Fat Food.

When the busyness of life reaches a crescendo, the wise cook falls back on food that can be cooked without coddling. While many dishes are soothing and self-sufficient, the one-pot meal is a harried cook's salvation. When you are too busy to think about food but you know you will be starving at the end of the workday, one-pot meals are the answer. They are helpful and agreeable—and practically cook themselves. All they ask in return is occasional stirring.

Traditionally, one-pot meals are winter food: hearty and filling. You can dress them up with a loaf of good bread, a salad, and fruit for dessert. Through the generations, cooks have come to rely on such classics as chili, chicken pot pie, pot roast, soup, corned beef, and spaghetti. Initially, these meals require a flurry of preparation—chopping, mixing, searing, sautéeing. Then you can sit back and relax, rousing yourself every thirty to forty-five minutes to lift the lid and see what's going on. An unwatched pot can burn or boil dry. Once, memorably, I neglected a pot of boiling beef and nearly burned down my kitchen. When it comes to slow cooking, forgetful souls—and those who are prone to boil-overs and fires—should drop a kitchen timer into their pockets, and then *pay attention* when it dings.

A one-pot meal is for homebodies. However, they are not for exhausted cooks. When you are frayed and weary, the thing to do is have food brought to you—pizza or take-out Chinese. But for cooks with plenty of energy and no time, one-pot meals can be a salvation.

The ultimate creation is pot roast. I can't say enough nice things about this dish. It is patient, tolerates myriad ingredients, and doesn't mind a little neglect. The cut of beef is negotiable—chuck, bottom, rump, brisket, sirloin. I buy what's on sale.

I know many recipes for pot roast, but my favorite came from my father's sister, Joyce Forbes, who is a marvelous Southern cook. She gave me the recipe at my father's funeral, when the talk settled on food—specifically how to cook when time is limited. Aunt Joyce said she had the perfect solution. The dish took all day and required little hand-holding. Aunt Joyce starts her roast in the morning, letting it simmer while she goes to Mass. Then she sits in her kitchen with her friends, and they spend the rest of the day playing *bourrée*, a sort of Cajun poker game. By five o'clock, the roast is done. With French bread, a tossed salad, and fresh strawberries for dessert, Joyce has a feast.

Aunt Joyce's Biloxi Pot Roast
Yield: 8 to 10 servings

Salt and pepper a 3- or 4-pound chuck roast, then dust with paprika. In a heavy, well-seasoned cast-iron Dutch oven, heat 2 tablespoons olive oil. Sear the roast on all sides. Aunt Joyce says to nearly blacken it, just shy of burning. The point is to get a really crisp, brown crust on the meat. Next, add 1 chopped yellow onion, 2 minced cloves garlic, and 1 cup chopped celery. Then add 1 cup red wine and 8 drops of Tabasco. Cover and cook on a low flame all day, say, from 8:00 A.M. until 5 or 6 P.M. After three or four hours, take a fork and break up the meat (it will naturally shred).

This is a versatile dish that works with your schedule. All the roast requires is an occasional check, to make sure that nothing is burning or sticking to the pan. An hour before serving, add 1½ cups bottled barbecue sauce (if you're in a rush) or your favorite homemade recipe (made a few days in advance, to enhance the flavors). Serve on French baguettes or buns.

You can vary this recipe by skipping the barbecue sauce. After the meat has cooked an hour or so, add some peeled carrots and potatoes, cut into chunks. The result is a cross between pot roast and stew. You can't go wrong with this recipe. Finicky souls can pluck out the carrots.

The slow cooking disintegrates the chopped onion and celery—slipping by the pickiest of eaters. The children can drink milk, and the adults can sip pinot noir. If a small-town society columnist was invited to your dinner, she would write: "A splendid meal was enjoyed by all."

Diana Gabaldon's Mahacha
Yield: 6 to 8 servings

If you are looking for something with a Southwestern flair, then *Mahacha* is the perfect dish. The recipe was given to me by Diana Gabaldon, a bestselling novelist who also happens to be a busy wife and mother. She inherited the recipe from her father, the late senator Tony Gabaldon, who was a marvelous cook. It's not unusual to find Diana prowling in her kitchen at 2 A.M., making chicken enchiladas for a child's school party, or whipping up a batch of curried chicken and pineapple salsa for a dinner. When she told me about *Mahacha,* I thought it was a twin to Aunt Joyce's Biloxi Pot Roast. It's not. *Mahacha* belongs in a category by itself. And it can be made in stages, which is a blessing when time is short.

Instead of searing the roast in oil, Diana boils it for 4 or 5 hours, depending on the poundage. Any cut of beef will do. Take care not to let the beef boil dry, as I once did—setting off the smoke detectors and ruining my favorite Dutch oven.

A word about boiled beef. It is the ultimate one-pot meal. In *More Home Cooking,* the late Laurie Colwin described her method of boiling beef. She pepped up the water with veal bones, dried porcini, garlic, a carrot, and one onion studded with peppercorns and a clove. For the finicky, the herbs and spices could be collected in a bouquet garni. Rather than boil the beef on a stove top, Laurie Colwin baked hers in a 300-degree oven for 3 to 5 hours. If you are inclined toward fires, this is the preferred method. The broth freezes beautifully.

For *Mahacha,* skip the dried mushrooms, step up the garlic, and throw in a whole hot pepper pod. A bay leaf is a nice touch, along with a handful of cilantro. But don't make a fuss. When it comes to *Mahacha,* plain water is fine; and if you are rushed, it's mandatory. After boiling, chill the roast overnight (or all day). When you are ready to cook, shred the meat with your fingers, taking care to remove the excess fat. Meanwhile, chop 1 onion, as much garlic as you like, 1 red bell pepper, 1 green bell pepper, and a handful of cilantro. Throw everything into a heavy skillet. Cover and cook on a low flame, adding a spoonful of water now and then to keep the meat from sticking to the skillet. Salt and pepper to taste. Use the filling for tacos, burritos, or enchiladas. Heap on grated Jack cheese; heat in the oven (350 degrees for about 15 minutes) or the microwave. For a festive touch, pass a bowl of chunky salsa. Sprinkle the burritos with extra cilantro and chopped green onions. Hoard the leftovers. I have been known to eat this cold at 3 A.M. with red-hot salsa.

Southwestern food lends itself to fabulous one-pot meals. When the weather turns cold and damp, I love the ritual of fixing chili. The dish itself is congenial yet passionate, arousing strong opinions about recipes and techniques. Trey is my firstborn son, and even before he became a chef, he made marvelous chili. He says it helps to drink a little beer while you are chopping ingredients for this dish—just watch your fingers. He ought to know. He works at a little cafe in South Carolina. One day he was chopping vegetables; the knife slipped and he put on a Band-Aid and kept chopping. During the lunch hour, a customer screamed. She reached into her spinach salad and pulled out a bloody Band-Aid.

Trey's Chili
Yield: 6 to 8 servings

INITIAL PREPARATION

1 green bell pepper, chopped
1 orange bell pepper, chopped
1 red bell pepper, chopped
4 stalks celery, chopped
1 bunch green onions,
   chopped
1 large onion, chopped

1 teaspoon minced garlic
8 slices bacon, chopped
   (optional)
1 teaspoon olive oil plus 1
   teaspoon unsalted butter, if
   needed

Wash and prepare your vegetables. This seems like a large amount to chop, but it's part of chili-making. Just watch your fingers. In a large skillet, over medium-high heat, cook the bacon. Remove with a slotted spoon and set aside. Reserve for another use. Add vegetables and sauté in the bacon drippings—if the vegetables seem a little dry, add the olive oil and butter. When the onions are translucent, add 1½ pounds ground round and 1 pound sirloin steak cut in 1-inch slabs. Brown meat. Remove meat and vegetables with a slotted spoon, draining as much fat as possible, and set aside.

Into a large, heavy pot, put 1 jar sun-dried tomato sauce and 1 jar roasted sweet pepper sauce, 3 large cans diced tomatoes, cut up, 3 table-spoons tomato paste, 1 teaspoon paprika, and 2 tablespoons chili pow-der. Pour in ¼ cup tequila. Add the meat, sautéed vegetables, and 2 cans chili beans, rinsed. Add 1 can water. Bring to a boil, then reduce heat and simmer 3 hours.

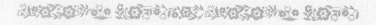

Chili is almost too casual for company; it's also territorial—people have staked out their own special recipes, using cumin or fresh basil or a splash of Corona. Most people are good-natured about it, but a few are pigheaded. Once, at a neighborhood chili cook-off, two grown men got into a fight and fell into the swimming pool. Naturally you don't want your chili to antagonize your guests; if you serve chili to a crowd, expect everything from cheers to criticism. But take heart. If you serve it in the kitchen, dishing it straight from the pot, you'll disarm the nitpickers. Beer also helps. Pass jalapeño corn bread, or just eat crackers from the box, and don't forget to bake a huge pan of scratch brownies for dessert.

୧୨ ୧୨

My paternal grandmother was born on Avery Island, and her daddy helped process the peppers for Tabasco. He was the head of Southern Shell Sea Food—and the first man to successfully can crabmeat. I remember him as a jovial, bald man of German descent, who had married into a French clan in southern Louisiana. As my mother said, "They lived to cook." To this day, Mama still prepares a dish that was my father's favorite, an incomparable one-pot meal. In my great-grandmother's kitchen, it was served with a pot of long-grain rice, a green salad, and fresh French bread, which was used for sopping up the "red" sauce.

Grandma Wagner's Smothered Steak
Yield: 4 to 6 servings

PREPARATION

1 large onion, chopped	¼ cup chopped parsley
1 clove garlic, minced	1 small can tomato paste
½ cup chopped celery	1 teaspoon brown sugar
½ bell pepper, chopped	(optional)

Have the butcher cut a 3-inch-thick round steak.* In a heavy, deep, cast-iron pot, heat 1 tablespoon olive oil. Brown the roast on both sides. Remove to a platter and set aside. Add the chopped vegetables to the pot and sauté until the onions are translucent. Add the tomato paste. Save the can. Keep stirring, letting the paste cook a bit. Add a teaspoon of brown sugar, if desired. Return steak to the pot. Using the empty tomato paste can, add 2 cans water (or 1 can water plus 1 can red wine). Cover the pot and cook 5 to 6 hours, stirring periodically. Serve with long-grain rice and lots of French bread.

*Allow ½ to ¾ pound of meat for each person. I have used rump, round, and chuck steak.

꿍 ꒒

When pork tenderloin goes on sale, I rush down to the market. Although technically not a pot roast, a tenderloin can be prepared in a single pan. If you use a Dutch oven, you can sear the roast in a little olive oil, then smother it in wine, chopped onions and garlic, and red bell peppers and cook it in a 350-degree oven. If you add potatoes and carrots, you have a whole meal in one pot. Start your roast early and go about your business. You don't have to worry about the pot boiling dry. The dry heat of the oven works magic on the roast—while it cooks, you can work in your attic office. When the aroma winds its way up the stairs, into the peaked roof of your hideaway, you know it's almost time to eat. This is the sort of meal I prepare when the cook needs coddling. Count on having leftovers. Lay in a supply of sandwich fixings—bread, lettuce, pickles, tomatoes, and Dijon mustard. Two ¾-pound pork tenderloins will yield 6 servings.

Comforting Pork Roast
Yield: 4 servings

Season a 4-pound loin of pork with lemon pepper, thyme, paprika, freshly ground pepper, and salt. Heat 1 tablespoon olive oil in a large sauté pan and sear the roast. After browning on all sides, put the meat in a large roasting pan. Deglaze the pan with ½ cup red wine. Then add 1 chopped onion, 3 stalks chopped celery, and 1 clove garlic, minced. Pour over the roast. My mother and I bake a 4-pound pork roast for 2 full hours at 350 degrees, but my son goes strictly by the internal temperature of the roast. When the meat thermometer reaches 135 degrees, his roast is done. As a registered nurse and worry wart, I can't bring myself to use his method. When the meat's internal temperature reaches 160 degrees, not *one* dot lower, my roast is officially done.

Pork lends itself to honey-mustard glazes and pear-and-port sauces. Last Easter, my son rolled a tenderloin in a pecan-herb crust, which was ambrosial. If you require a side dish, throw in a few new potatoes and let them roast in the pan juices. Baby carrots are also quite agreeable with pork. But if you really want to be fancy, make a cherry salsa.

Ary Jean's Cherry Salsa

Yield: 1½ cups

⅓ cup chopped onion
⅓ cup chopped green pepper
⅓ cup chopped green chiles
⅓ cup dried cherries, chopped

1½ tablespoons champagne
   vinegar
1½ tablespoons chopped
   cilantro

Mix. Spoon over the roast. On a cold, rainy night in October, this meal is dignified and delicious. With a loaf of French bread and an upside-down apple cake, it's downright festive. Savor the complex flavors. Marvel at the simplicity of it all. Brag that this recipe allows the impossible—the cook can be in two places at the same time. While the roast cooks, you can hang curtains, pitch a ball to your child, or write a story. It doesn't get any better than that.

The Side-Dish Dilemma

When it comes to side dishes, never underestimate the salad. Although some people would never dream of calling it a side dish, a simple green salad can be a cook's best friend. Aside from being time-efficient and easygoing, it is good for you. There is nothing lazy or inappropriate about a meal that features grilled flank steak, a plain green salad, and garlic bread. Technically this is a meal without sides, but only the most haughty palate would complain.

—Cousin Jeannie, aka Beverly, discussing side dishes at a Paris cafe, 1993

I grew up on blue-plate specials—known in cafe lingo as a meat, bread, and two sides. Every night we sat down to an orchestrated menu. We ate fried pork chops with mashed potatoes and pan gravy, snap beans from the garden, fried apples, and corn sticks; pot roast, pan potatoes and carrots, egg noodles sprinkled with poppy seeds and fresh parsley, gravy, and yeast rolls. When my grandfather sent fresh shrimp from the Gulf to Tennessee, we'd have a seafood boil, accompanied by corn on the cob, slaw, potato salad, baked beans, and lots of French bread. Usually there was banana pudding or chess pie for dessert.

The perfect side dish does not demand coddling, prayers, or a silent kitchen. Ideally, it requires the same amount of cooking time as your chosen entrée—or, preferably, it can be made ahead of time. My Mimi used to say that side dishes travel in pairs; one dish usually supports and enhances the other, like potatoes and carrots, cabbage and carrots, or potato salad and baked beans. Sides look best on the plate if you have varied the colors; a monochromatic scheme must be avoided. Once I thoughtlessly cooked an all-white supper: creamed chicken, mashed potatoes, parsnips, biscuits, cheesecake.

Last Easter, when my older son was home from chef school, he cooked a pork tenderloin accompanied by a pear-and-port sauce. For dessert, he served poached pears. Ideally, he would have liked a romaine salad with a pear vinaigrette. He says one flavor should echo throughout the menu, permeating the meal yet not dominating. Textures should also be taken into consideration.

I blame home economists for the obsession with side dishes, but in the fifties, motherhood confused food with love; in some cases, it was served as a substitute. Baby boomers were plied with meat loaf, scalloped potatoes, green beans, yeast rolls, chocolate cake. As a result, when a boomer steps into the kitchen, he (or she) feels compelled to produce side dishes. My husband is a boomer who expects a full meal. He was raised with a blue-plate mentality, too, featuring the plainer side of cafe cookery. No garlic, not a drop of Tabasco, and a heavy hand with salt, bacon grease, and lard. When we were first married, he would step into the kitchen and eye the meal—usually baked chicken, steamed broccoli, and store-bought rolls. "Is this *all*?" he'd ask.

"What do you mean, all?" I'd cry.

"I'm just checking to make sure I'm not missing anything," he'd say.

In an attempt to satisfy my husband's appetite for the four food groups, I have been driven to concoct vegetable casseroles. Many of the recipes involved canned cream of chicken (or mushroom) soup, water chestnuts, and a can of French-fried onion rings. One summer I toyed with soufflés, but motherhood left me with little time, not to mention a houseful of little boys slamming doors—not suited to the soufflé, which requires silence.

Anyway, these casseroles all had a fussy edge. My husband picked at them, and the boys refused to eat them at all. They were reminiscent of dishes my mother served at bridge luncheons. As I scraped the casserole into the trash, it seemed to me that embellishing a vegetable is a little risky—like dressing a cat in baby clothes. The only difference is, the vegetable won't hiss at you. It just sits there, allowing you to smother it with hollandaise, sour cream, or Campbell's soup.

Most household menus revolve around an entrée: roast chicken, sautéed crab cakes, grilled tuna, and so forth. The harassed home chef can usually be found on the kitchen floor, surrounded by cookbooks, casting about for harmonious "sides." The candidates can be overwhelming. Any Junior League cookbook is full of vegetable dishes: rice pilaf, eggplant Parmesan, creamed onions. Broccoli Supreme, prepared a thousand different ways, is a favorite party dish. My dog-eared copy of *The Memphis Cookbook* (Junior League of Memphis, originally published in 1952) features five different squash casseroles, along with something called "Peas à la Bonne Femme," which I've been too cowardly to make. The *Pastors' Wives Cookbook* by Sybil Du Bose suggests a dish called Carrots Lyonnaise, involving chicken bouillon cubes, and Carrots en Sauce, which calls for horseradish and a whole cup of mayonnaise.

The modern cook is not blessed with leisure time. A chaotic lifestyle demands simplicity. Don't kid yourself—an orchestrated meal requires planning, experience, and a sense of timing. When you pull your meat loaf from the oven, the potatoes should be freshly mashed, the beans tender and piping hot, the corn bread freshly buttered. And you have to consider likes and dislikes. There's no sense in making jalapeño potatoes if no one will eat them but you and the dog. As a child of a child of the Depression, it worries me to waste food.

Nevertheless, I do find myself inventing campaigns for certain vegetables, usually if I secretly adore them. I am devoted to Brussels sprouts, but my family hates them. I have smothered sprouts in butter, concealed them in cream sauce, and doused them in a vinaigrette. Then I would shamelessly lie to my children. "Hey, guys," I'd say, holding up the dish. I'd usually pick one of the Limoges bowls for the occasion. "Guess what we're having tonight? Little cabbages!" I figured it had worked with broccoli— "little trees," I called them—but the boys shook their heads.

Every few months, when I get a sprout craving, I sit down with my cookbooks and try to find an appealing recipe. I found a stunning candidate in John Thorne's *The Outlaw Cook*. It involves steaming the sprouts for about seven minutes—you don't want to overcook them. Slice and sauté in a little butter or olive oil. While the sprouts gently brown, throw in bread crumbs and a handful of cheese. John Thorne suggests freshly grated Parmesan, but I love hot-pepper cheese. Homemade bread crumbs take this dish to a higher realm.

Down home, traditional side dishes include potato salad, baked beans, and an array of squash casseroles. Seasonal sides are dependent on the local produce—fried okra, snap beans, butter beans, tomatoes, peppers. Corn is versatile. It doesn't mind being fried, roasted, boiled, or slashed off the cob. And all cooks are familiar with the potato's virtues. Not only is it a workaholic, it is a shape-shifter, a master of disguise. It can be scalloped, baked, fried, sautéed, boiled, and shredded into pancakes. If it weren't a vegetable, it would make a marvelous spy. A favorite company dish is:

Jalapeño Potatoes
Yield: 6 to 8 servings

1 small green bell pepper, chopped
1 small onion, chopped
2 cloves garlic, minced
2 tablespoons unsalted butter
4 medium red potatoes, sliced (peeling is optional)
One 2-ounce jar pimientos, drained and chopped
½ cup (1 stick) plus 2 table-spoons unsalted butter

1 tablespoon all-purpose flour
1 cup milk
Half a 6-ounce roll garlic cheese
Half a 6-ounce roll jalapeño cheese
Salt and pepper to taste
2 cups bread crumbs (optional)

Preheat oven to 350 degrees. In a frying pan, sauté the bell pepper, onion, and garlic in the 2 tablespoons butter. Grease an oblong 3-quart baking dish and add, in layers, the sliced potatoes, the sautéed vegetables (bell pepper, onion, garlic), and the pimientos. Keep layering until all the ingredients are gone. In another frying pan, melt the ½ cup butter. Stir in the flour and keep stirring until the flour and butter are blended and lightly browned. Slowly add the milk. Next, add the cheese. I couldn't find any jalapeño cheese, so I substituted 6 ounces of hot-pepper cheese. Salt and pepper. Pour this cheesy mixture over the potato mixture. Top with homemade, buttered bread crumbs. Bake 45 minutes.

Some foods are harmonious. Consider the cabbage: It is, to my mind, a polygamous vegetable, rather like the aunt who has been married five times and she's still man-crazy, a little too eager to please. It's a congenial partner for almost any entrée. While it is fond of carrots and potatoes, the cabbage doesn't mind if you chop it into a slaw, mixing it with mayonnaise, onions, and bell peppers. Potato salad is another congenial side, especially when it's paired with fried chicken or baked ham. Deviled eggs are perennially appealing, although they aren't considered an official side outside the South.

A basic cream sauce, which is incredibly easy to make, lends a little glamour to vegetables. In a skillet, melt 2 tablespoons unsalted butter. Add 2 tablespoons all-purpose flour and ½ teaspoon salt. Whisk. Remove from heat and slowly add 1 cup milk, whisking constantly. Return to heat and simmer for a minute or two. (Yield: 1 cup.) This sauce is marvelous over cauliflower, sprouts, asparagus, and new potatoes (with a bit of fresh parsley sprinkled over the top). And once you master the cream sauce, you can make béchamel by substituting 1 cup chicken stock for the milk; then sprinkle in a little paprika and gently add ½ cup cream. For a caper sauce, add 3 teaspoons chopped capers and 1 teaspoon lemon juice. A cheese sauce can be made by adding ½ cup grated cheddar.

The sweet potato is a controversial side dish. Although it has defenders, most people seem to despise it. A sweet potato is a sweet potato, no matter what you do to it. In certain culinary circles, the sweet potato has become fashionable, even trendy. Southerners find this amusing; the sweet potato has always been considered a traditional holiday side dish. My uncle Ponchatus used to bake them in the fireplace, right in the ashes. And every Thanksgiving and Christmas, my Mimi baked them with Karo syrup and marshmallows—a loathsome dish, in my opinion. Even as an adult, cruising down the produce aisle at Kroger, I avoided sweet potatoes.

Then, in the early eighties, I went to my cousin Lula's for Thanksgiving, and I reversed my opinion about this root vegetable. Lula is Dell's baby sister, but they couldn't be more different. Lula is not only a four-star cook, her house is organized and immaculate. She keeps falling in love with offshore oil barons. When her daddy died, all three of Lula's ex-husbands showed up at the funeral home. It caused quite a stir. They held her hands and fetched hot coffee and produced handkerchiefs, waving them under her nose like white flowers.

At the Thanksgiving dinner, Lula kept passing dishes. One bowl featured a burnt orange substance, all crusted with pecans.

I suspected that it might contain sweet potatoes; it smelled spicy, with a tinge of maple candy. Lula's casseroles should be enshrined, and many have graced the pages of Junior League and church cookbooks, so I wasn't going to be a coward. I found an empty spot on my plate, between the oyster dressing and the smoked turkey. Then I stuck a silver fork into the concoction and took a bite. An ambrosial taste filled my mouth—why, it was almost like a pudding, yet savory.

"What *is* this?" I asked Lula; but in my heart I was thinking: Please don't let it be sweet potatoes.

"Sweet potato soufflé," she said. "Isn't it fabulous?"

I nodded, then took another serving. I was hooked. Since then I have cooked this dish many times, and even sweet potato haters will compliment it.

Cousin Lula's Sweet Potato Soufflé
Yield: 4 to 6 servings

2 cups cooked, mashed sweet potatoes (canned is fine)
1 cup granulated sugar
2 eggs, beaten
1 stick unsalted butter, melted

½ cup evaporated milk (I use Pet brand)
½ teaspoon ground nutmeg
½ teaspoon ground cinnamon

Preheat the oven to 400 degrees. Whisk all the ingredients together and pour into a greased 2-quart baking dish. Bake 20 minutes. Remove from the oven and add the topping.

To Make the Topping

1 stick unsalted butter
1 cup brown sugar
1 cup crushed cornflakes

½ cup chopped pecans
10 pecan halves

Melt the butter; add the sugar and cornflakes. Stir. Spoon over the potato mixture. Sprinkle on the chopped pecans. Dot with the pecan halves. Return to the oven and bake 10 minutes longer.

Side dishes don't require a pedigree. Recently I served my mother and brother frozen Italian-cut green beans—cooked with a small ham hock, a pinch of sugar, and a whole hot red-pepper pod. "Did you can these?" they wanted to know. When I admitted the beans were frozen, Mama made me fish the bag from the trash can. "I'll never plant another bean," she declared. "I'll just cook frozen."

When it comes to choosing side dishes, always remember that simple, unadorned vegetables can be compelling. A steamed artichoke is a lovely thing. And nothing beats a baked potato. There are few things more elegant than asparagus, steamed with a little lemon juice and a sprinkle of kosher salt. The nutty, complex flavor is a joy on the tongue. And a cut-glass plate full of sliced, homegrown tomatoes, still warm from the sun, is ravishing.

Picky eaters can severely limit your repertoire. However, don't be afraid to flirt with vegetables. You never know when you might find something you adore. The best place to search for sides is in a vegetable cookbook. Many years ago, during a spate of vegetarianism, I bought *The Enchanted Broccoli Forest* by Mollie Katzen. Now I keep it beside my bed, to peruse on sleepless nights when side dishes haunt me.

Sometimes I leaf through church cookbooks. In one book, twelve different women submitted the same recipe for Broccoli-

Rice Casserole. It called for frozen broccoli, cream of mushroom soup, dehydrated onion, Minute rice, and Cheez Whiz. As Miss Johnnie used to say, "Forget the sass and steam that broccoli, child."

Amen.

How to Season Cast Iron

All the mysteries of Southern cooking can be solved in an old black pot.

—Aunt Joyce Forbes, champion *bourrée* player and divine Cajun cook

Like most Southerners, I grew up watching the women in my family produce gourmet meals in cast-iron pans. The skillets were the color of unlit charcoal, with a slick, hard finish. They were stored in the oven; the deep kettle usually emerged in time for Christmas gumbo, lingering into early spring for savory stews. I never questioned my relatives about their cookware. I knew that the pans, like our food and our men, were "well seasoned"; as far as the patina that Mama treasured so much, I assumed it more or less occurred on its own.

Over the years, I had inherited many pieces of cast iron, seasoned by the excellent cooks in the family. I am sorry to say that I did not appreciate these pans. I stashed them in a deep cupboard and forgot about them. Then one spring my husband presented me with a brand-new, ten-inch skillet—and he challenged me to season it. First, I called Mama, who said to stick the pan in a fire.

"Isn't there an easier method?" I asked her, wondering where I'd build a fire in my backyard.

"I've never seasoned a pan," she admitted.

"I'll call you later," I said. The instructions suggested rubbing shortening in the pan, then gently heating it. Thinking this would be a snap, I smeared the inside of the pan with Wesson oil. Then I set it on the burner. Thirty minutes later, the pan was still gunmetal gray. Next, I put the pan in the oven. After a two-hour stint at 350 degrees, the results weren't satisfactory. In the bottom of my skillet was a sticky film, and several places appeared gummy. My pan wasn't black—it was still gray.

Assuming the pan was seasoned, I set out to cook scrambled eggs—a big mistake. The eggs not only stuck to the pan, they seared into the iron itself, becoming a permanent part of the metal pan. Taking my usual approach to burned-on food, I filled the sink with hot, soapy suds and soaked my skillet overnight. True, I'd never actually seen my mama wash her skillet, but I praised myself for being clever—leave it to the modern cook to utilize the overnight soaking method.

The next morning, I ran to the kitchen and peered into the sink. I almost wept. My skillet had rusted. When I lifted it from the reddish water, the scent reminded me of old garden tools, the type that have been left out in the rain for a hundred years. Convinced that I'd ruined my pan, I called home and explained the situation.

"You crazy young girls," my mama said, laughing. "I don't see why you want to use cast iron when you can buy All-Clad."

"Yes," I said, "that's easy to say, because *your* pans are seasoned. Anyway, I want to see if I can do it."

"I'll give you a pan," she said, "if you stop torturing yourself with this oil-and-bake business."

The trouble was, I was beginning to see the seasoning process as a challenge. Cast iron has been around for thousands of years, and I wanted to make my own little heirloom, something a little more meaningful than Teflon to pass down to my children. I longed for a Dutch oven, a twelve-inch skillet, a chicken fryer, and a mold for corn bread sticks. I told myself that cast iron was healthy, a sneaky source of dietary iron. Sure, I could find a pre-seasoned pan at Mama's house or the local flea market, but I wanted a hands-on transformation.

Cast iron has many virtues, but seasoning isn't one of them. It requires time, oil, and an oven. Store-bought pans come with instructions, but they skip over all the important parts—the same way intuitive cooks gloss over recipes, assuming you know that T. stands for tablespoon and not teaspoon. And be forewarned: Buying cast iron is a commitment. You are taking on a project. One or two hours of "curing" won't create a black, nonstick pan. I hate to tell you, but *six* hours won't do it either. Be prepared to spend time with your purchase. Most all instructions tell you to apply oil and bake for X hours or minutes. They don't tell you that seasoning is acquired slowly, like maturity. You'll have to oil and bake for many hours, when your time and schedule allow you to cook an empty pan. At times it will seem as if you are serving up nothing; you'll wonder how many centuries it will take before your pan acquires a rich, black patina.

"How long?" I asked Mama, biting my nails.

"Years," she said gloomily. "Like forty or fifty."

The first step is so simple that many people skip it—washing the pan in soapy water, using a scouring pad. This is the one and only time your skillet will *ever* have intimate contact with soap. Scrub hard—you're removing the protective coating that inhibits rust. It's important to remember that unseasoned cast iron is relatively fragile, so take care not to drop it on the floor, and high temperatures can actually warp the metal. After drying the pan, you're ready to start seasoning.

During the curing process, the oil hardens to a "varnish"-like finish. The pan gradually loses its gray color, turning progressively browner until it attains the famous black "crust." I grew to love the fragrance of an empty, slow-cooking skillet. It made my house smell old-fashioned and metallic, the way water smells when it trickles from an iron pump. If you don't like the aroma of baked iron, you can close off your kitchen or burn a vanilla-bean candle. The scent of oxidizing metal reminds me of meals past and meals present, a whole heritage of women who conjure food to feed their loved ones. If nothing else, seasoning is the perfect activity for people who spend many hours at home, whether they are raising small children or writing novels. Once, my husband came home, sniffing the air. "What's for supper?" he asked hopefully.

"Tuna salad," I said.

"Oh. Well, it sure smells good," he said, looking confused. I didn't explain, and the salad was a hit, especially when I served it with homemade rolls.

After you've washed and dried your pan, you're ready for the next step: oiling. This is not the time to be sloppy or fainthearted. Finicky souls use a pastry brush; earthy people prefer their fingers. I myself use a paper towel, all scrunched up, then doused with oil (although I have been known to pour oil directly into the pan, about 2 teaspoons, then swish it around with a paper napkin, taking care not to leave little flecks of lint). Now take the oily paper towel and rub inside the skillet. Cast iron is somewhat porous, and it will absorb the oil. Get into every little crevice—hold it up to the light, making sure you haven't missed a spot. The motto of cast iron is less is more, and this is especially true when it comes to oil—thin coats are best. I don't oil the outside, but some cooks slick down everything, including the lids and handles. Put your pan in a 275-degree oven for about five hours, periodically checking to see if you need another coat of oil. Think of it as a slow layering, the way an artist layers colors on a canvas. After a couple of five-hour sessions, you'll begin to notice a metamorphosis. You'll know when you're making progress: Your pan will acquire a thin, hard layer; it resembles shellac—shiny and transparent, the color of caramel flavoring, and faintly tacky.

Now is a good time to explain about the oiling process. The type of oil is debatable—some cooks swear by safflower, some prefer Crisco. (In the olden days, people used lard.) I have talked to women who detest corn oils, claiming it leaves a residue. My mother swears by olive oil, but I myself have had good results with peanut oil—it has no discernible flavor and it's stable at high temperatures. Whatever you decide, don't use salted butter. And remember to use small amounts—I can't stress this enough. Otherwise, your skillet can develop sticky splotches. This happened with my second pan, a small skillet, and I didn't understand what I was doing wrong until it was too late. Some cooks believe that this gummy stage is the beginning of the curing process, but there's a difference in coats. A slightly tacky, amber sheen means you're making progress, but a sticky sediment, one that literally sticks to your fingers, means you've used too much oil.

If you've already got a half-seasoned pan, one that's sticky in places and seems to attract stray cat hairs, don't worry—there's a cure. Merely scrunch up some waxed paper and lightly buff the pan. If you've really gone overboard with the oil and have large amounts of goo, scrub the pan with a little sea salt and a Tuffy pad. Take care with this method—you might remove more than the stickiness; in the early stages of curing, the patina is some-what delicate and requires coddling.

There are many methods to season cast iron, but the main for-mula seems to be vegetable oil plus heat equals patina. I've heard of people turning their pans upside down in the oven; many cooks use the stove-top method, coating the interior and gently heating the pan until it just starts to smoke. I tried this once, and it set off my smoke alarm.

Cooks also disagree about temperatures and baking times. A number of people cure pans at higher temperatures, say 350 to 400 degrees, to speed up the evaporation of the oil. (I have done this myself with semi-cured pans, using olive oil and a 375- to 400-degree oven. A small amount of smoking occurred at tempera-tures over 400 degrees; however, in about three hours my pans were noticeably darker.) Paul Prudhomme cures his new pans with low heat, about 225 degrees, leaving them to bake for hours.

My mother, another Louisiana cook, swears by this method, too. She suggests hastening the process by adding a little salt, letting it slow-heat in the pan. The best pans of all, she claims, come from relatives or garage sales.

Achieving patina takes the patience of a saint and the finesse of a landscape painter. Try to think of it as an adventure. Curing is nothing more than basic kitchen chemistry: The multiple oilings, when combined with heat, fill in the microscopic "pits" in the cast iron. Over time, these pits harden, producing a smooth, black surface. The oil actually creates a barrier, preventing oxygen from reaching the iron and causing rust; it also forms a virtually nonstick surface. I have a chicken fryer that's been baked almost ten hours, and it still isn't the characteristic black—it resembles caramel-colored iron with a thin, clear coating of burnt sugar. The patina of my Dutch oven is still a mere baby. The more you use the pans, the more they will blacken, eventually losing the raw metallic color.

When the time comes to clean your pan, remember this rule: Never soak, never scour. A sink full of soapy water can undo years of care. A friend in Florida cooked beef-and-mushroom stew in her flea-market skillet. While she was in the shower, her mother thoughtfully washed and scoured the pan. When my friend emerged from her shower, her mom held up the pan—as shiny as a tenpenny nail. My friend screeched, then broke down and wept. The seasoning was completely destroyed, and my friend's pan still isn't right, even though she has spent hours trying to reseason.

Despite this cautionary tale, there are people who swear by

detergent and water, but I remain wary. If you are going to the trouble of owning cast iron, raising it from infancy, the least you can do is protect it. When you are faced with a grubby skillet, it helps to think of the cleaning as a ritual. Hold your pan under hot running water, using a Scotch-Brite or Tuffy pad (never use steel or copper or you'll be sorry). Do not even *think* about using soap or steel wool. You aren't washing the pan as much as "sanding" it—gently honing the little bumps, making the surface as smooth as a baby's bottom.

Unless you are fond of rust, thoroughly dry your pan; some cooks put their skillets into the oven to dry out. After it's cooled, wipe down the surface with the barest coat of oil—do this every time you use the pan for the first year. A paper towel patted down over the skillet seems to inhibit rust in humid areas.

Points to Remember
- It is wise to keep one skillet just for making corn bread and upside-down cakes. Use a second pan for frying.
- However: Try not to go cast-iron crazy—it is unwise to have four or five uncured pans lying around the house. Aside from being dust magnets and taking up cabinet space, each pan requires a lengthy break-in period—and maintenance.
- No soap, no scouring!
- Never wash in a dishwasher—it will rust your pan and remove the seasoning.
- Until your pan is seasoned, try not to cook sticky things— sometimes it causes setbacks.

- Clean with hot water and an abrasive nylon pad, sanding the surface.
- After cleaning, dry the pan thoroughly. For the first year, lightly oil. Store in a dry place.
- If scrubbing is needed, sprinkle kosher salt into the skillet. Use a Tuffy pad to gently—or vigorously—scour.
- For heinous messes, heat the pan with a bit of water and simmer. Using a stiff brush, scrub the burned-on residue. Remove from heat, rinse under hot running water, using a Tuffy scrubber, if necessary. Dry, then set in a warm oven.
- The acidity in tomatoes can have ghastly consequences in cast iron, unless you are using other ingredients, like in a stew or spaghetti sauce.

One last recommendation—until your pan develops a smooth, nonstick finish, use it wisely. Everything will want to stick. Once I fried chicken in a skillet that had been cured for only four hours. I was left with a dense, crusty ring that seemed to permeate the metal. I scrubbed and scrubbed. Later, I wiped on oil and baked it for about five hours, just to regain the lost coating. Because using the pan enhances the seasoning process, try cooking innocuous things, like grilled sandwiches (minus the cheese), using a bit of olive oil (I have known bread to stick to half-cured skillets—this is not a pretty sight).

Now that you've painstakingly oiled and seasoned your skillet, protecting it from soap and moisture, it's time to cook. Until your newly seasoned pan acquires a little age, I wouldn't use it for a béarnaise sauce (probably All-Clad is best for delicate creations), but it's perfect for sautéeing onions, celery, and garlic. By the time you are pan-frying T-bones, you'll never look back.

As you set the table with your grandmother's Fiesta dishes, picture your stash of cooking catalogues, especially the ones that feature cast iron. Now you are ready to order muffin tins shaped like cacti, roses, or tiny catfish. Soon, very soon, you'll be ready for a *beignet* fryer. Remember that cast-iron cookery is part art, part science, but mostly it is an ancient culinary method. Pat yourself on the back because you've been patient; you've fretted and coddled and oiled and baked. Remember that you aren't just cooking supper in your cast iron—you are seasoning your pan. You are also creating an heirloom, a piece of culinary history to pass down through the generations.

Funeral Food

Live and learn. Die and get food. That's the Southern way.

—Anonymous casserole enthusiast, on her way to the mayor's funeral, Cookeville, Tennessee, 1995

In small towns, after a death, it is traditional to bring covered dishes to the family. When words fail us, we offer food. A platter of fried chicken says, *I'm sorry for your loss.* A chocolate layer cake whispers, *I know you feel that life has soured, so here is something sweet.*

In church lingo it is called "food for the bereaved." Southern churches have traditionally provided the meal after the funeral; it can be grand or pathetic. And you can't go by a church's size, either—even though church kitchens are built to feed the multitudes. Nowadays they are professionally outfitted with six-burner stoves (electric, most likely), convection ovens, and walk-in pantries. When it comes to good funeral food, it all depends on how many good cooks are in the congregation.

Even the funeral home anticipates the culinary hodgepodge. The undertakers thoughtfully provide the family with a little booklet, a food log to jot down the donor's name, offering, and description of the plate. They even provide gummed stickers to affix to the bottom of dishes, so each one can be returned to its proper owner. All funeral food is acknowledged with a thank-you note. The dishes are washed and promptly returned to the donor (although I know a family in Texas who received so much food it took them eight months to return all the bowls). My mama says the returning of dishes forces widows and orphans to get dressed and crawl out of their shells; after a spell of grieving, it is therapeutic to visit with friends.

Taking food to the bereaved always throws me into a panic—what to prepare? Food lore suggests that eggplant helps the grieving soul come to terms with endings. Zucchini is also a comfort food, and poppy seeds are said to induce sleep. Other cultures literally bring food to the dead. In Mexico, the deceased's favorite foods are brought to the cemetery and left on the grave. A burning candle sheds light on the feast, leading the recently departed to his earthly delights.

Funeral food has a few unwritten rules. It must transport with ease, and be reheatable. Spicy foods should be avoided. Choose dishes that comfort the broken-hearted, entice blunted appetites, and satisfy the nongrieving relatives—distant kin who, for various reasons, always seem to gather at funerals. They come in four types: the curious, the dutiful, the greedy, and the reluctant. This last group consists of children and preteenagers who have been dragged to the event. One thing never changes: They all want food, and plenty of it.

After a death, fried chicken is usually the first dish to appear on the bereaved's table. I've often thought it would be interesting to do a comparative study of funeral chicken. Some crusts are flaky and crisp, the color of mahogany; others are pale brown and damp, with the consistency of wet toilet paper. Still others clearly come from KFC. My friend John Myers recently lamented the passing of good church food. At a family funeral, his mother's church brought fried chicken from Hardee's. John was aghast, especially since this was the Deep South, and for decades, his mother had been supplying the church with jugs of sun tea, baked hams, and potato salad. In her basement was a whole set of funeral dishes, with her name scrawled in laundry ink on the bottom of each pan.

In addition to fried chicken, typical funeral fare ranges from baked ham to rump roast to pit barbecue. Other dishes include deviled eggs, potato salad, coleslaw, cheese grits, macaroni and cheese. Large quantities of sweet tea are usually available. Crock-Pots always show up at a funeral, usually filled with green beans or a roast. A dozen Jell-O salads will materialize, spread out on the table like quivering jewels. Some are sweet, with marshmallows, nuts, and canned fruit; others are savory, with mayonnaise, chopped celery, and olives.

The casserole will make an appearance at every funeral dinner. Hot chicken salad topped with crushed potato chips is a perpetual favorite, along with a broccoli-and-chicken concoction. Chicken and dumplings fall under the category of old-fashioned funeral food, but it takes time and effort to prepare. Chicken pot pie is another funeral dish that's fallen out of favor, probably because it's best eaten the same day it's cooked, otherwise the crust suffers.

If the death occurs in the summer, when gardens are producing, someone is bound to bring a platter of sliced tomatoes. Squash casserole is a favorite dish, along with simple bowls of peas, snap beans, and fried corn. Any time of year, a platter of sandwiches is appealing: egg salad, tuna, ham, chicken, roast beef. For breakfast, a pan of sweet rolls, with a sprinkling of pecans, can soothe an anguished heart. Every church usually has a home baker who supplies yeast rolls, sausage and biscuits, and corn bread (although I have begun to see an influx of store-bought rolls).

At the home of any bereaved soul, you will find extravagant desserts, mostly pies and layer cakes. This is a time when home cooks bring their specialties. The pies are typical Southern holiday fare: lemon icebox, chocolate, coconut, pecan. In the South, chess pie is also known as funeral pie:

Lemon Chess Pie
Yield: One 9-inch pie

PREPARATION

1½ cups sugar	2 teaspoons fresh lemon juice
1 stick unsalted butter, melted	1 teaspoon vanilla
4 eggs, beaten	

Preheat the oven to 325 degrees. Cream together the sugar and the butter. Add the eggs and blend well. Add the other ingredients. Pour into a 9-inch unbaked pie shell. Bake 40 to 50 minutes, until set. Test by inserting a knife toward the pie's center; if it emerges clean, the pie is ready. This basic recipe cries out for tinkering. If you want to make a chess coconut pie, add 3½ ounces flaked coconut. If you dislike lemony pies, substitute 1½ teaspoons vinegar. For buttermilk pie, omit the lemon juice and add 1 teaspoon all-purpose flour and 1½ cups buttermilk. If anyone asks why it's called chess pie, explain that old Southern cooks used to keep their pies in a chest, or safe. The doors of the chest were made of perforated tin to allow air circulation.

Pound cakes and sheet cakes are also popular offerings. They are quick to bake and easy to transport. Sometimes the simplest desserts are the most pleasing: a yellow Bundt cake with a plain confectioners' glaze is a soothing thing to feed a child. Banana pudding, usually made in a round Pyrex bowl and topped with two inches of meringue, is an eternal favorite. Lemon squares, piled up on a cut-glass plate, will make you smile—they are cheerful and soul-lifting, the culinary equivalent of spending time on a sunporch. My mother used to say that a lemon square, served with a cup of hot tea, revives the spirit. It's a recipe that requires a little effort, but it pays you back tenfold.

Lemon Squares
Yield: 16 bars

TO MAKE THE CRUST

1 cup all-purpose flour	⅛ teaspoon salt
1 cup confectioners' sugar	1 stick unsalted butter, cut up

Preheat the oven to 350 degrees. In a large bowl, sift together the flour, sugar, and salt. Using a pastry blender (or two knives), cut the butter into the mixture until it is crumbly. Press the dough into a greased 9-inch square pan. Bake 15 to 20 minutes. The crust should be lightly browned.

To Make the Filling

3 large eggs
1 cup granulated sugar
1 tablespoon lemon zest, finely chopped
4 tablespoons fresh lemon juice

2 tablespoons all-purpose flour
½ teaspoon baking powder
⅛ teaspoon salt

In a large bowl, beat the eggs until blended. Add the sugar and blend. Add the zest. Gradually stir in the lemon juice. Sift the flour, baking powder, and salt into the egg mixture and blend until smooth. Pour the mixture over the crust. Bake 25 minutes. Cool on a rack—do not remove from the pan.

To Make the Topping

1½ cups confectioners' sugar
3 tablespoons lemon juice

Mix sugar and lemon juice. Spread over cooled filling. When the icing sets, cut into squares.

Some food is inappropriate for the bereaved. This is not the time to bring Better Than Sex Cake or Death by Chocolate. And it's never a good idea to use uncooked eggs in funeral food. For instance, butter-cream frosting is easy to make and outrageously delicious, but it calls for raw egg yolk. This can be dangerous for the very young and the elderly, or anyone suffering from immunosuppression. If your famous chicken salad recipe calls for homemade mayonnaise, you might want to substitute a commercial brand.

It is wise to consider the effects of grief on the gastrointestinal system. During times of stress, the body is delicate. Also, depending on the geographical region, it's probably not wise to bring a platter of stuffed jalapeños or *anacuchos*. Even something as ubiquitous as chili might throw the digestive system into a tizzy. Personally, I think a tongue-burning salsa would be a welcome distraction from mourning, but in sensitive souls, the jalapeños might produce reflux, better known as indigestion, which feels like a powerful heartache. A stressed-out person might confuse the pain with angina, resulting in an unnecessary trip to the emergency room.

Another improper funeral dish is baked beans. At first glance, this classic food seems to fulfill the criteria of bereavement cuisine: It's easy to make, easy to transport, and feeds a thong of guests. But this dish is traditionally hard on the gut. Unless you lay in a supply of Beano, flatulence will most certainly result, and this condition is not welcome in closed-up houses and funeral parlors. The results have been known to incite bitter family quarrels.

I myself have never seen appetizers at a funeral. And I have yet to see chicken soup. You'd think it would be just the thing to take the edge off grief: It serves a crowd, it's a snap to reheat, and it possesses amazing powers to console and cure. However, it sloshes while being transported. Unless you bring it in a huge Tupperware bowl, the poor widow, who is already distracted by grief and guests, will have to find a great big pot to reheat the soup. Unless a kind neighbor is pulling kitchen duty, the widow has two pans to wash—yours and hers.

Mashed potatoes is the ultimate comfort food, but no one ever shows up with it at wakes. For all its virtues, meat loaf hits the wrong notes; but I'm sure it has been offered—and devoured. I

Cooking Lessons

have never seen beef stew, liver and onions, or hamburgers brought to the bereaved—but I'm sure it's been done. Many years ago, I brought a piña colada cake to grieving teetotalers, with my name carefully taped to the bottom of the pan, and my cousin Lula once brought bourbon balls to a deacon's widow.

For those of us who can't think of anything appropriate to say or cook, my mother suggests bringing paper plates. After a funeral, or in the days preceding one, someone is always eating, and the last thing a widow needs is dishpan hands. It is also a good idea to provide plastic forks, knives, and cups. Napkins are thoughtful. A pound of freshly ground coffee beans will be put to good use, along with Styrofoam cups, sugar cubes, packets of Sweet'n Low, and a jar of Coffee-mate. My mother once said that coffee seems to be the beverage of choice after a death. I have never seen wine or beer brought to the bereaved's house, although on some occasions a tiny nip of something stout, like Jack Daniel's or Wild Turkey, might be just the thing.

When you bring food to a neighbor or a friend, you are wisely letting the food fill in the gaps. Sometimes we say all the wrong things, but food knows all languages. It says, I know you are inconsolable. I know you are fragile right now. And I am so sorry for your loss. I am here if you need me. The bringing of food has no denomination and no race. It is concern and sympathy in a Pyrex bowl. In the kindest sort of way, it reminds us that life continues, that we must sustain and nourish it. Funeral cuisine may be an old custom, but it is the ultimate joining of community and food—it is humanity at its finest.

Chicken Soup and Other Cures

1. Eat when you feel hungry.
2. Sleep when you are sleepy.
3. When nature calls, answer it.
4. When it's cold, go inside.
5. Don't think of anything else while making love.

—Dr. Irving Oyle's "Guide to Good Health," from *Chop Wood, Carry Water*

My family has always been into home remedies. Whenever my brother or I caught colds or the flu, Mama would drag out the black iron pot and make chicken soup. She would serve it in china gumbo bowls, set on tole trays, accompanied by flat 7UP and a stack of saltines.

I trusted that soup, even though I wasn't sure how it worked. Evidence is largely anecdotal, but it seems to me that a steaming vessel of fluid is just the thing to soothe clogged respiratory passages. Also, garlic—a key ingredient in Mama's broth—is reputed to have antibacterial properties. Some doctors believe that chicken broth is an excellent fluid replacement. Hospitals use intravenous solutions with 5 percent glucose and water, but normal saline seems to be the infusion of choice. And it is nothing more than salt water, which is the basic component of amniotic fluid and the sea.

Therapeutic Chicken Soup
Yield: 10 to 12 servings

PREPARATION

3 chicken breasts with bones, skins removed

8 stalks celery, chopped

2 medium onions, chopped

1 red bell pepper, chopped

½ green bell pepper, chopped

4 to 5 cloves garlic, minced, *and* 2 tablespoons minced garlic from a jar—more, if you dare

4 tablespoons chopped fresh parsley

2 to 3 tablespoons chopped fresh thyme

3 leeks, chopped (use the white part)

4 to 5 carrots, peeled and sliced

3 potatoes, peeled and cut into chunks

6 to 8 cans chicken broth or equivalent amount of homemade stock

3 tablespoons paprika

Juice of one lemon

1 tablespoon sugar

Kosher salt, freshly ground pepper, Accent, Tabasco— to taste

Combine the ingredients. Simmer 2 hours, uncovered, on a medium-low flame. During the last hour, reduce the flame and simmer, covered. If desired, boil ¼ to ½ box of fettucini or orzo (prepare according to the directions on the package; boil in a separate pan). Drain; add pasta just before serving.

This soup is aromatic and herbal. The chicken breasts are easier than stewing a whole chicken—you don't have the fat and dark meat to discard. Canned stock doesn't seem to interfere with the therapeutic properties. The hardest part is chopping the vegetables—especially if you are running a temperature. But once you've chopped everything, you can coast. With saltine crackers, this soup is a full meal.

In addition to curing humans, this soup has been known to cure dogs. Last fall one of my Scotties, Scout Louise, became gravely ill. The veterinarian was perplexed. A blood test revealed dangerously high liver enzymes. A cursory auscultation of the chest detected labored respirations, possibly fluid in the lungs. The vet started an intravenous infusion in her neck. Then he announced he was giving her Lasix. At this, I protested—Lasix is a powerful diuretic. True, I'd graduated from nursing school twenty years earlier, but some things never change. The combination of intravenous fluids and Lasix seemed contradictory. I challenged the vet, and he blustered about housewives and a little bit of knowledge being dangerous, assuring me that he knew best. "Your dog will probably die," he said.

I took Scout Louise home and made her a pallet beside my bed. Then I spoon-fed her Gatorade and warm chicken soup. The next morning, she'd perked up enough to notice the cat. By the second day, Scout chased the cat into a silk ficus tree. I never found out what ailed the dog, but I found a new vet.

One thing is certain—when you are suffering with a cold or the flu, chicken soup acts like a tonic. Frequently, the ailing person is too feverish to make soup. If the patient lives alone, or lives with individuals who aren't handy in a kitchen, there's still hope. Even a child can make a tonic.

Estelle Brabham's Flu Tonic

Chicken broth (any quantity; canned is fine)
5 cloves garlic, crushed
Tabasco, 5 dashes

In a saucepan, combine the ingredients. The quantities of garlic and
Tabasco are negotiable. Bring to a rolling boil. Remove from the heat.
Serve in a large mug.

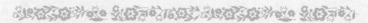

A favorite family remedy concerns sinking spells. While this
ailment is not a bona fide illness, a sinking spell is characterized
by lethargy. It ranges from mild to severe, and appears to be
hereditary. Although not much is known about this malady, a
sinking spell can be preceded by a migraine, an allergic reaction,
or a broken heart. It usually occurs when you are mentally and
physically exhausted—after funerals, or when you've been up all
night with a colicky baby. You flop on the bed, too tired to kick off
your shoes. The spirit is willing, but the body refuses. You long to
take a nap, but you can't. Supper must be cooked, the laundry
needs folding, and your oldest child must be driven to soccer
practice. For a mild boost, squeeze ½ lemon into a glass of water
and drink slowly. Tougher cases require a more complex cure.

How to Reverse a Sinking Spell

When you feel under the weather, and your heart is about to
break, peel ½ inch of a fresh gingerroot. Then grate the ginger
into a saucepan. Add 10 slices of fresh ginger, peeled or unpeeled.

If desired, flavor with a little brown sugar. Boil twenty minutes. Strain. Pour the ginger tonic into a pot of freshly brewed Lapsang souchong tea.

I won't lie: This can be a vile drink. But it's good for you. It can make you grimace and stomp your foot, but it's bracing, surprisingly savory, and curative. Serve in delicate china cups. Close your eyes and wait for the reversal to begin.

Consuming
Passions

Old-Fashioned Louisiana Love Potion

If you experience erotic or gastric difficulties while enjoying oysters, consult a qualified professional.

> —Disclaimer, found on a sack of oysters, somewhere in the French Quarter, 1998

Yield: 1½ cups

PREPARATION

1¼ cups chili sauce
3 tablespoons fresh lemon
  juice
3 tablespoons prepared
  horseradish

2 teaspoons Worcestershire
  sauce
Jolt of Tabasco

Blend all ingredients, stirring until smooth. Chill one hour. Serve with oysters on the half shell, taking care not to swallow a pearl. Oysters are best eaten during an R month—otherwise, they can be milky. But try and tell that to a true oyster lover.

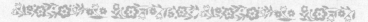

During the seventeenth century, a rumor got started that oysters were aphrodisiacs. Possibly it was just a biochemical reaction when the lover boy (or lover girl) was faced with a cold, fleshy oyster—one look, and the bloodstream was flooded with adrenaline. Another rumor claimed that if you combined oysters and caviar, the libidinous effect was deliciously magnified. I myself think that is a rumor worth investigating.

The common oyster makes its beds from southern Maine to the Gulf of Mexico. And luscious oysters are harvested in Tomales Bay, in northern California. All along coastal America, right at this moment, people are sitting down to oysters on the half shell. I grew up believing this was a Southern food, but an old beau set me straight. The Yanks have been eating oysters for centuries, he told me. In the early 1800s, oysters were so plentiful in Connecticut you didn't have to get your feet wet to harvest them.

Four hundred years later, oysters are still considered the food of lust. Ask anyone, and they'll tell you that raw oysters can cure a sagging libido. Perhaps this is sheer myth. One thing is certain: Oysters are low in calories, high in iodine and zinc. If you are fortunate to know a person who can wield an oyster knife, treat that person well. He is practicing an art form.

Whether your passion is Lindt chocolate, French champagne, or raw oysters, you are in good company. Casanova ate over four dozen bivalves a day (along with vast quantities of chocolate— another aphrodisiac). He supposedly put a raw oyster in his mouth and slipped it between the lips of his *belle de jour*. Imagine her shock. Imagine her pleasure.

Slick and sensuous, tasting of the sea, the oyster arouses strong emotions. Some people are born slurping them straight from the shell. Others think the taste is acquired, and a few cynics think the love magic is simple: If you'll eat a raw oyster, you'll eat anything. Whatever you believe, just close your eyes, open your mouth, and don't forget to pass the sauce.

The Quest for "Q"

Many Southern passions have risen to prominence beyond the Mason-Dixon line: Krispy Kreme doughnuts, Blenheim ginger ale, and pit barbecue. At a New York rib joint, it's elbowroom only. And a stampede occurred during the opening of a Manhattan Krispy Kreme.

—Margaret Jane Campbell, Southern scholar and foodie

In 1962, my family spent a week in Florida, feasting on fried shrimp and raw oysters. On the way back to Tennessee, my mama said, "I never thought I could get tired of seafood, but I am. I'm craving something meaty."

As my father sped down the highway, Mama took a poll, and everyone in the car—which included my father, my brother, and me—agreed we needed something to settle our stomachs. "I know just what we need," Mama said. "Pig meat. Kids, start looking for signs."

This was before the days of interstate highways in the South. We were traveling down a rough paved road, a major thoroughfare that was lined with billboards and hand-painted signs—"Burma-Shave," "Peaches for Sale," "Pecans by the Pound." It wasn't long before we found a crude sign, "Pit Bar-b-que," featuring a smiling pig surrounded by a halo of orange flames.

"Turn, Ralph!" cried Mama, shaking his arm. "See that sign? Turn down this road. No, no. *This* road, the one next to the bait shop."

My daddy turned. His motto was: Woe to the traveler who leaves a rough paved road in the South, but worse woe to the driver who doesn't listen to Mama. She can get loud. In all of our travels, she has led us down some weird byroads. A few years earlier, she'd followed a sign to a farmhouse that sold us poisoned sausage, and we all ended up in a Georgia emergency room.

I'm sure my daddy was thinking of this as he aimed the Buick down a curvy two-lane road. The tires sent up a plume of red Alabama dirt. I rolled down my window, hoping my nose would pick up the scent, but all I smelled was pine and swamp water. Now and then, a crude sign would loom up: "BBQ This Way"; "Bar-B-Cue, Five Miles"; "Q: Keep Going." Not only did the signs feature different spellings, some offered different mileages. We drove a long way and spotted a new sign, which urged us to keep going a few yards farther. My daddy clocked twenty miles on the odometer, an unheard-of distance for a pork sandwich. Mother laughed nervously, and ran one hand through her short, curly hair. "I think this pit is somewhere over the rainbow," she said.

I spotted another sign: "bAr-BeE-QuE, 2 mIle aHeAd." "How many feet in a mile?" I asked.

"That depends on where you are in Alabama," said Daddy, and Mama punched his arm.

We drove an interminable distance, stopping once for gas at an ancient Sinclair station, with the green dinosaur on the sign.

"Haven't seen a dinosaur in years," Mama said. "Maybe we entered a time warp."

My brother and I exchanged glances. It was possible. Mother was a lively storyteller. Her tales were vivid; we did not question the authenticity of any story. We had come to believe that she'd lived through much of the Old and New Testaments, and had intimate knowledge of the Dark Ages, the Renaissance, and the Civil War. We believed she had been on the *Mayflower,* that she'd been with Scarlett the night Atlanta burned.

Daddy was standing by the pumps, asking the attendant for directions to the pit. The man just waved at the road and said, "It's just on down a ways a bit."

Mama leaned across the seat. "How far is a bit?" she asked.

"Not far," said the attendant.

We paid for the gas and headed back onto the red dirt road. Daddy muttered that we'd gotten turned around and were heading for the coast of Georgia. "I'm starting to smell salt water," he said.

"Hush," Mama said. She stuck her head out the window and drew in a deep breath. "I smell it. Hickory! Turn here, Ralph! Right down this gravel road."

"But there's no sign," Daddy cried, scratching his bald head.

"Trust me," said Mama, leaning out the window again. "It's just got to be down here."

We drove another mile or so, stopping once to let a possum cross. At long last we pulled up to a blackened concrete building, set way back in the loblolly pines. We looked all around the parking lot, but there was no sign. Still, we knew we had found the right place. From the roof, a chimney emitted a stream of fragrant smoke. We looked at it reverently. The smoke hung in the air, a delicious fallout that instantly set our stomachs to growling.

Scattered about the parking lot were banged-up trucks and cars—a good sign, Daddy said. We climbed out of our Buick, slapping at our wrinkled clothes. Out in the lot, the scent was stronger. As Mama said later, "The piquant aroma nearly knocked us flat!" We rushed toward the rusty screen door, flung it open, and charged inside.

This was a real joint, offering sandwiches and no "sides." If you needed something to wash down your sandwich, then you had to dig through the cold-drink case. The joint offered five different sauces, but Mama said that the best pit-smoked barbecue should stand alone. The flavor of the meat should be savored, chewed slowly, accompanied by guttural sounds—lots of "mmmmms" and "hmmmms."

To this day, I slam on the brakes when I see a barbecue sign. And whenever I descend into the cellar at the Rendezvous in Memphis, I start trembling, because I know what's coming. Even the pickles taste good at the Rendezvous. On hot afternoons, while driving to the beach, I always stop at a roadside pit in Alabama. I step inside the squatty building and take a seat at a plank table, folding my hands as if praying; but I'm really trying to decide if I want the pork pulled or sliced. Like many Southerners, I can become downright evangelical over cuts of meat and sauces. I'm always telling my Yankee friends that the South is a place of fire and brimstone barbecue. Some folks might even argue that a BBQ belt exists alongside the Bible Belt.

Like Protestants, "Q" comes in many denominations: beef or

pork; wet or dry; sliced, pulled, or chopped. But the meat is only one burning question. Saucing is a major concern, influenced by lore and local tastes. To some, it's an obsession. There are many concoctions, all highly regional, each one vigorously defended by its inventor.

The three fabled sauces—vinegar, mustard, and tomato—have a thousand variations. There's the peppery vinegar sauce, as thin as rainwater, that prevails in the eastern Carolinas; moving farther south there's the tangy mustard sauce of the low country; the fabled dark red tomato sauce holds sway in Memphis—it's my hands-down favorite; there are the fruit-juice marinades—orange and honey—in Florida "Q"; the spicy Cajun influence brings a depth to Louisiana pork meat, and Tabasco adds fire. Farther west are the mesquite rubs of Texas; the chili peppers of the Southwest; and the influence of the Orient in California "Q"—sauced with soy, honey, rice-wine vinegar, and ginger.

Some folks insist on eating their barbecue "neat"—pure meat piled up on white bread. A few hard cases ask for a tongue-blistering pepper sauce, and others prefer plain ketchup. Die-hard Tarheels like to insult Memphians, calling the sauce "tomatoey no-account Delta barbecue." It's all what you're accustomed to. Since barbecue grew out of an era without electricity, in a region where pork was readily available, food historians believe that vinegar was used as a preservative. Others contend that it was used to mask rotten meat. Still, the rivalry continues, making "Q" as diverse as the South itself.

One weekend I gathered up some friends and took a "Q" tour, sampling every barbecue pit in the Memphis area. Armed with a list of famous and infamous places, we took our time, drinking a little beer to clear the palate. We were searching for the Nobel Prize of sandwiches: pulled vs. chopped vs. sliced; vinegar vs. mustard vs. tomato vs. "neat." Of course, all platters and "sides" were sampled, too. By the end of the weekend, we'd each consumed about 50,000 calories, and it was years before we could look at coleslaw.

My own mama was fond of food excursions. When my father was alive, they often took theme trips—melons, sausage, peaches, shrimp, pecans, and ice cream. She claims that she has literally eaten her way through the South. Barbecue was her favorite touring food. She always said that good "Q" is food set to music—a rumba, maybe, or a country ballad. It depends on the region.

Truth be told, many Southerners don't know how to barbecue. The younger generation confuses grilling with barbecuing, which is blasphemy. Short of digging an actual pit in the backyard, which is never a fun thing to do, a portable smoker is an admirable way to get home-style "Q." Just be sure what you are smoking.

Once I sent my husband to the market with instructions to buy a Boston butt or a pork shoulder. He came back with a small cut of meat. Then he threw it into our backyard smoker—a Brinkmann, bought on sale at Wal-Mart; when it's really smoking, it looks very much like R2D2, the little droid in *Star Wars*. I always love to stand back and watch: Smoke makes barbecue seem mysterious and clandestine. Many a young woman has been seduced after an evening of torrid barbecuing.

We cooked the meat all day, adding dampened chunks of hickory wood. The smoker has a little pan of water that sits under the meat and catches the drips. My brother always pours a bottle of Wick's marinade over his meat, with the residue falling into the drip pan. As the water sizzles and evaporates, it flavors and tenderizes the meat. Some cooks inject the marinade into the meat, others baste with a giant paintbrush.

Because smoking is a long process, we used an old grill as a "nursery" for the charcoal, transferring the briquettes to the smoker with tongs. By the end of the day, our clothes and hair reeked of hickory. An old pit master had advised me to smoke for twelve hours, minimum; but halfway through the process, the meat turned very, very black, and I was forced to wrap part of it in tinfoil.

Mama spoke up and said, "Let your husband tend that meat. Pit-mastering is a man thing. It's the perfect activity for them."

"Isn't that a little sexist?" I asked.

"Why, indeed not! It keeps a man occupied for eight to ten hours. Honey, that's an all-day vigil. And the wife can go about her business—or mischief. But the man can't. He's stuck."

Eight hours later, as I started to "pull" the meat, I noticed it was pink, almost blood-colored. "Why, it's raw," I thought. Then I looked closer. It was ham! My husband had gone to the market and bought a picnic ham, not a pork shoulder!

"I didn't know the difference," he confessed. "Did you?"

"Doesn't matter," I said, popping a strand of meat into his mouth. "It's ambrosial. I think you're onto something, Will."

"The sky's the limit," he said. "Next time I might buy a whole pig."

"Don't get too grandiose," Mama said. She reminded me of the time, years ago, when we took Trey, my eldest son, to a steak house. He looked up at the waitress and said, "Ma'am, does the prime rib come barbecued?"

Now that child is a chef, and a barbecue connoisseur. He says that when it comes to genuine pit barbecue, one thing is certain: Good joints are never franchised. Excellent "Q" takes time. It involves getting up at three A.M. to add fresh wood—and good wood is frightfully expensive. This is horrible news for people who live outside the South, but even commercial barbecue is better than none at all. Whether it is roasted in a charcoal smoker or slow-cooked in a pit, barbecue is a taste of the South. It's a noun, a verb, and an entire religion served on a bun: pig meat, chopped or pulled, with or without sauce. Roll up your sleeves, grab a pile of paper napkins, and wait for manna from Heaven.

How to Make Perfect Iced Tea

I make tea in my Mr. Coffee pot. A thing of water and four tea bags does the trick. After the water runs through, I shut off the pot and add a cup of sugar.

—Anonymous slob, sitting on a mall bench somewhere in
Atlanta, discussing beverages with another slob, 1996

Growing up in a region where appetites and thirsts are legendary, I have come to believe that iced tea is the basis of Southern living. My grandmother used to say that this beverage runs through the veins of any native Southerner. I believed her. As a Louisiana baby, I was served coffee and tea, mixed with cream and sugar, in my glass EvenFlo bottle. Even now, forty-something years later, I have a profound weakness for the brew. My screened-in porch is a favorite drinking spot, but it also doubles as a dining/family room, while the summer night gently darkens around us, like tea that has steeped too long. Add a couple of eccentric relatives, preferably Southern, and wait for the stories to begin. All Southern tales are like intricate recipes—part myth, part truth, and part lies.

To make a perfect jug of tea, you need more than boiling water and a tin of leaves. First, supply the background. A large wooden porch, preferably screened, is a nice beginning. Add wicker chairs and at least one wooden glider. A mild breeze, especially if it carries the scent of charcoal or freshly cut grass, is especially welcome. Flowers, such as nasturtiums and violets, either floating in the tea glass or anchored in a lemon round, lend an exotic touch (if you find yourself inclined in that direction). Add one Southern orchestra—crickets, katydids, and bullfrogs—and you are well on your way to perfection.

There is nothing more comforting than the sound of warm tea poured into thin, ice-filled glasses. Understand that tea making isn't complete until you own a small collection of pitchers. Clear, simple jugs are always lovely, but on special occasions bring out your cobalt and cranberry glass. As you pour, remind yourself that antique glassware enhances the depth and beauty of tea, not to mention your afternoon, especially when you add lemon, mint, and a lace-edged napkin. On especially muggy nights, press the cold, wet glass to your forehead. Hold a glass to the light, admiring its rich colors of citrine and topaz. Expound upon the virtues of iced tea—cold and tart, warm and plain, sweet and tangy, spiced and spiked. It's versatile, generous, eager to please, the perfect beverage for any meal. (Also, it's nondenominational.)

In the Deep South, tea drinking commences immediately after breakfast (or however long it takes you to drink three cups of coffee). Walk barefoot into your kitchen, letting the screen door slam behind you, and measure two cups of cold water. Pour into an enamel pan and turn up the flame. When the water begins to smile (as the French say), remove the pan. Add two family-size tea bags and cover the pan for ten minutes. Purists will stick to plain tea—unsweetened and unadorned, but I myself crave a bit of sugar. And no matter how it's served, tea fits into any menu or season. It's the backbone of summer, especially when served with pecan chicken salad and garden tomatoes. In the fall or winter, its character changes with the addition of spices and heat. I have a tattered sheaf of recipes for "Russian Tea," but I prefer a steamy cup served English-style, laced with sugar and a splash of cream. Cointreau adds depth and zing.

Most people make iced tea without thinking—indeed, they're puzzled when you ask them for a recipe. Nevertheless, the perfect brew eluded me for years. In a world of complicated beverages, tea making is utterly fundamental. Even a child can make it. Most cooks don't measure; they just draw up a pan of cold water, bring it to a boil, drop in a few tea bags, and steep. Maybe they'll shake in sugar, straight from the bag (certainly they won't use a measuring cup, with its increments marked off to the nth degree).

My grandmother Mimi did not have a cookbook-lined kitchen; her cuisine was a product of instinct and memory (Mimi was the biscuit-making daughter in a family of ten children—the second-oldest sister was the hair braider, and she went to her grave without learning how to make a decent pot of tea). I remember shopping with Mimi at Central Grocery in New Orleans, across the street from the French Market. I doubt that she knew that tea fell into three basic groups: green, oolong, and black. Still, she knew what she liked: Earl Grey, with its elegant, sweet, and fruity blend. Darjeeling, with its mild taste, a close second. The man at the grocery explained that pekoe referred to the size of the leaf, not the flavor, but looking back, I really think he wanted an excuse to sidle up to my pretty grandmother. As she bought Lapsang souchong, garlic braids, and muffuletta, Mimi told me to always remember that men liked robust flavors. She was speaking of the Mississippi "chaps" from her youth—men who accompanied their women to the Amite River Baptist Church, but in their minds were hunting quail from Thanksgiving Day until Christmas. In her generation, Southern women worshiped the menfolk. The men ate together in the dining room, circled and coddled by women. "Get you another biscuit," they'd say. "Honey, don't gulp that down. There's extra pie in the safe. All you want."

My grandmother understood that men are as variable as tea leaves. Some are gentle, subtle; others are bland like weak coffee. They can be cloudy and mysterious, too hot or too cold. Now and then you find one who is acidic—a bitter lemon ruining the flavor of your whole brew. You have no choice but to throw it out and start over. And some men, bless their hearts, are downright sweet. You can't help but love them a little more than the others.

My grandmother also believed in the excellence of tea leaves; she eschewed prepackaged bags. "Would you dream of using instant coffee?" she'd scold when I'd reach for a plastic-wrapped box in Piggly Wiggly. "Tea leaves are to tea what fresh perked is to coffee." Well, that made sense. Even though it seemed troublesome to strain her brews, she never used a tea bag in her life.

After my grandmother passed away, my mother became the official "tea maker" in our family. While she confessed to using store-bought bags, she always used a quality black tea. She also confessed her secret technique—part science, part hocus-pocus.

Although tea water must be boiled in order to bring out the flavor, she never lets her water boil very long (she claims it causes the water to taste metallic). And she never reboils water.

My mama claims the sort of pot one uses to boil the tea water is important. Aluminum is forbidden. She recommends stainless steel, glass, or enamel (although I remember when she served tea in those wide-lipped aluminum tumblers, the kind that came in jewel-toned colors and made me shiver when my teeth touched the cold metal rim). Recently she has taken to serving all beverages in lovely etched goblets made of the thinnest crystal, and it seems as if we are drinking liquid jewels. While cranberry glass and crystal provide a certain atmosphere, the foundation of my mother's tea is a sugar syrup.

How to Make a Sugar Syrup
Yield: Sugar syrup to sweeten 1 quart tea

Into a saucepan, put 1½ cups sugar and 2½ cups water. Stir over low heat until the sugar is dissolved. Gently bring to a boil. Boil ten minutes or until the mixture is reduced to a thick syrup. Cool. Pour into steeped tea (made with about 2 pints water). Add lemons, if desired.

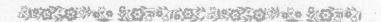

Basic Sweet Tea
Yield: 1 quart

2 pints water
2 family-size tea bags
¾ to 1½ cups sugar (omit if
  using a sugar syrup)

Sliced lemon rounds, for
garnish

Bring the water to just a hint of a boil. Add tea bags, remove from heat, and cover pan. Wait five minutes. Add sugar to your favorite pitcher. Pour steamed tea over sugar and stir. My mother adds 1 small can of limeade and 1 small can of lemonade, reducing her sugar to ¼ cup (or less—sugar is a very personal thing, she says). Next, she adds lemons, limes, oranges, and fresh mint. She has been known to pour the whole brew into a silver punch bowl, adding gin and thus creating her famous La-Di-Da Tipsy Tea.

La-Di-Da Tipsy Tea
(Borrowed from Ary Jean Helton)
Yield: Approximately 25 servings

1. Make a sugar syrup; cool.
2. Pour into a cut-glass punch bowl.
3. Stir in the juice of 6 lemons, 6 oranges, 3 cups plain, brewed tea, and ½ bottle gin.
4. Let stand 1 hour.
5. Stir in 2½ quarts chilled carbonated water.
6. Freeze tea (with fruit juice) in ice cube trays. Add to the punch. Heaven!

In my mind's eye, food and art are inexorably linked. Both nourish the spirit. Both collide daily in my kitchen. As a young tea maker, my brews were too strong, sweet, bitter, cloudy. Only in middle age have I learned the art of tea making. It helps to relax and have fun, to enter your kitchen with abandon and a certain wickedness. Throw away those measuring cups and reach for your child's yellow cat mug, the one that holds exactly 1¼ cups sugar (if you are the sort of person who demands a sweet life). Understand that a less than perfect glass of tea isn't the end of the world—more than likely, it's drinkable. Remember the words of a famous Southern heroine—"Tomorrow is another day," especially when it comes to iced tea.

Bake Sales

The finest food in the South can be found at bake sales. Every November the Baptist church has its annual sale, and the locals load up on cakes and pies: pumpkin, mincemeat, coconut, and lemon chess. Then they go home, serve it all to the men, and pass it off as home cooking.

—Aunt Tempe, making bake-sale brownies with her daughters, 1965

On Saturday mornings, just before dawn, while the moon is starting to fall into the hollows, and when the grass is squeaky-wet, my mama is already awake. As she sips her last cup of coffee, she studies church bulletins and garage-sale ads; she is searching for bake sales, and when she finds one, she circles it in pink Magic Marker. When she is finished, the papers look bloody, as if they've been through a war. Like a four-star general, Mama plans her strategy, drawing up maps, sketching roads, drawing stars and Xs over the most promising sales. A bold pink line shows her route. She drinks her coffee, going over her itinerary, picturing her yellow kitchen packed with pies, cakes, and brownies.

Bake-saleing must be planned with care and cunning. Before she leaves the house, she pulls on heavy socks and tennis shoes, jeans that won't rip when she hunkers down. She pats her pocket—plenty of dollar bills and loose change, and a checkbook, just in case she runs out of money. Then she scuttles out to her car, a flaming-red convertible, and drives off, into the sunrise.

One week after my father died, I woke up and found my mama standing in her kitchen, a pocketbook slung over her arm. "I know you won't understand this," she said, "but I'm going to a bake sale."

"But the house is full of food," I said.

"It'll soothe me."

"Want me to come along?" I said.

"No, you're too slow." She opened the back door and darted out.

Over the years, she has bought coconut layer cakes, mincemeat pies, apple fritters, and peanut butter bars. Small wars flare up at these sales, usually when two women lust after the same dessert. Mama has seen society ladies snarl and slap faces. Once she spotted a millionaire's wife swapping price tags. The rules are simple: Show up early; haggle if a cake is overpriced; travel in fast-moving pairs; and if something catches your eye, grab it. You can always put it down when something better comes along. Woe to the indecisive shopper. And woe to the shopper with a small bladder. Mama won't make pit stops at the 7-Eleven.

One time we'd all gone fishing. It was a pleasure boat, not built for serious fishing, and my brother accidentally hooked Mama between the shoulder blades. He sped to the dock, and we loaded Mama into the car. On the way to the emergency room, she screamed, "Stop the car!"

My brother slammed on the brakes. "What's the matter?" he cried.

"I saw a sign," she said.

"Oh Lord," said my brother. I knew he was worried; I was, too. Maybe Mama's wound was worse than it looked. The hook could have struck a nerve or vital organ. Now she was hallucinating. "What sort of sign did you see?" he asked.

"Bake sale," said Mama. "Two miles ahead."

ᙔ ᙠ

When people love food, they will go to extremes. They seek out recipes, order weird entrées at restaurants, and study cookbooks. They telephone other food enthusiasts. But even fanatics take breaks. They run out of time, get tired of baking, go on fad diets, or fall into sinking spells. This is when bake sales come in handy. They are usually advertised in church bulletins, or with handmade signs tacked to telephone poles.

My mother's little town is famous for its food sales. The church-sponsored events are first-class—apparently the young women's clubs have fallen prey to mixes—with the PTAs taking second place. At a typical sale you can find brownies, cookies, layer cakes. But when church women start cooking, you'll find yeast rolls, pecan coffee cakes, three kinds of zucchini bread, banana bread, pound cakes, and myriad fruit pies. You can buy red-velvet cakes, German chocolate cakes; cakes decorated with confectionary sunflowers and cakes iced around plastic dolls. Sometimes the women drag out canned goods: jars of green-tomato relish, bread-and-butter pickles, and kraut. It's awesome and inspiring.

In the fall, when the air turns crisp at the edges, I begin dreaming about spice cake, a favorite at any October bazaar. Like all scratch cakes, it requires a little time to prepare, but it's a worthy way to spend an afternoon. While it bakes, the whole house fills with cinnamon and nutmeg—the scent of autumn itself.

Fall Spice Cake
Yield: One 9 × 13-inch sheet cake

1¼ cups all-purpose flour
½ teaspoon baking powder
½ teaspoon baking soda
½ teaspoon salt
1 teaspoon ground cloves
½ teaspoon ground nutmeg
1 teaspoon ground cinnamon
1½ sticks unsalted butter, at room temperature

¾ cup granulated sugar
¾ cup brown sugar
3 eggs
¾ cup buttermilk
1 teaspoon vanilla
1 cup pecans, chopped
¾ cup raisins presoaked in vanilla or lemon brandy (optional)

Preheat the oven to 375 degrees. Grease and lightly flour a 9 × 13-inch pan. Sift together the dry ingredients. Cream the butter and sugars. Add the eggs one at a time, beating after each addition. Add the dry ingredients alternately with the buttermilk. Add the remaining ingredients and blend. Bake 35 to 40 minutes. Frost with caramel icing when cool.

CARAMEL ICING

1 stick unsalted butter
½ cup brown sugar

2 tablespoons evaporated milk
1 cup confectioners' sugar

In a saucepan, combine the butter and brown sugar. Cook over a low flame for three minutes, stirring constantly. Gradually add the milk. Bring to a boil. Remove from the heat and cool. Add the confectioners' sugar and beat. If it's too thick, add 1 teaspoon milk.

Spread on the cake. If there's any icing left over, pour into a buttered pan. Sprinkle with pecans. Cool and cut into squares. It tastes remarkably like old-fashioned pralines.

In my family, whenever a chocolate sheet cake appeared, it was usually to soothe a broken heart, or to soften the impact of an impulsive thrift-shop purchase. It was not the cake of holidays, but a cake that cajoled and flirted, a cake that said, "Forget about your problems, sweetie. Come sit by me for a while." For generations, this cake has been flaunted at county fairs and bake sales, hauled to picnics and potlucks. It has soothed many wild hearts. Simple, reliable, and delicious, this cake travels well. And you ice it right in the nine-by-thirteen pan.

I remember helping my grandmama bake this cake after she'd backed her car into a tree. The recipe called for three eggs, and I'd go out to the henhouse, gathering eggs. Sometimes a hen would lay an egg, and her cackling would set off a chain reaction in the coop. I'd reach under each bird, feeling for her prize. This recipe was my grandmother's grandmother's recipe. Whenever I bake it, all of my forebears gather in my kitchen. Elizabeth taught Estelle to make this cake, and Estelle taught Mimi, and Mimi taught Ary Jean, and Ary Jean taught Michael Lee, and Michael Lee taught Trey and Tyler. Every time I break an egg, the spirits guide me. When I stir the batter, I am stirring up these kitchen ghosts. They bolster me; but most of all, they whisper in my ear a split second before the timer buzzes.

Brabham Family Chocolate Sheet Cake
Yield: One 9 × 13-inch sheet cake

2 cups all-purpose flour	3 eggs, lightly beaten
2 cups sugar	½ teaspoon salt
1 cup water	1 scant teaspoon ground
2 sticks unsalted butter	cinnamon
4 tablespoons cocoa	1 teaspoon baking soda
½ cup buttermilk	1 teaspoon vanilla

Preheat the oven to 350 degrees. In a big bowl, mix the flour with the sugar. Boil the 1 cup of water in a large saucepan. Add the butter and the cocoa. Mix until the butter melts and the sauce is thick. Pour over the flour-and-sugar mixture. Using a large spoon, blend well. Add the buttermilk, eggs, salt, cinnamon, baking soda, and vanilla. Mix. Pour into a buttered 9 × 13-inch pan. Bake 35 minutes. Cool 5 minutes and ice the cake in the pan.

CHOCOLATE ICING

1 stick unsalted butter	3½ cups confectioners' sugar
4 tablespoons cocoa	1 tablespoon vanilla
6 tablespoons milk	1 cup chopped pecans

In a saucepan, melt the butter. Add the cocoa and blend. Slowly add the milk, whisking. Remove from the heat, then add the confectioners' sugar. Beat. The icing will be grainy, almost lumpy. Beat in the vanilla and the chopped pecans. Spread over the cake. Work fast—the icing dries quickly. It's traditional to have a young assistant lick the pan.

A scratch cake is an emotional creation, thought to be superior to anything in a box. It is steeped in domestic rituals: measuring, sifting, creaming, beating, stirring. The procedure seems daunting; but as you study the recipe, adding up the long list of ingredients, you find yourself reading between the lines. Who dreamed up this recipe? Who served it and why? Was it a cake to impress a beau, to distract a husband, or to donate to a church bazaar?

Sometimes bought cakes have surprising ingredients. Last spring my mother bought a lemon Bundt cake, thinking she'd serve it at Easter and pass it off as her own creation. The whole family gorged on that cake; not a crumb was left. Since Mother does not own a Bundt pan, we grew suspicious. When we demanded the recipe, she confessed she'd bought it at a bazaar. "But I know exactly who made it," she said, reaching for the phone book. "She's in my Sunday school class." After she got the recipe, Mama arched one eyebrow. "You won't *believe* what's in it," she said. "It's too bizarre."

"What?" I asked. "Tell me."

"It's a mix," she said. "You know what Dell would call it—'a bizarre bazaar cake.'"

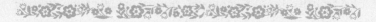

Lemon Cake
Yield: 10 to 12 servings

¼ cup fresh lemon juice
4 eggs, lightly beaten
½ teaspoon lemon extract
1 box Duncan Hines Lemon
 Supreme cake mix

One ³/₁₂-ounce box Jell-O
 instant lemon pudding mix
⅔ cup canola oil
½ cup chopped walnuts
Zest of 2 lemons

Preheat the oven to 350 degrees. First, make the lemon water. Pour the lemon juice into a large measuring cup. Then add enough water to make ⅔ cup. In a bowl, put the eggs, lemon extract, dry cake mix, pudding mix, and oil. Add lemon water. Beat on medium speed four minutes or until blended. Fold in the walnuts and lemon zest. Grease a Bundt pan, preferably with butter, and lightly flour. (Pam will work, too.) Pour the mix into the pan. Bake for 45 minutes. When the cake cools, dust with confectioners' sugar or make a lemon glaze.

LEMON GLAZE

¼ cup fresh lemon juice
1 teaspoon lemon zest

½ teaspoon lemon extract
1 cup confectioners' sugar

Whisk all the ingredients till blended. Using a wooden skewer, poke holes in the cake. Spoon the glaze over the cake. Serve this cake after a citrus meal—lemon-grilled chicken, and spring asparagus dressed with a little lemon juice and the tiniest dot of butter. You can dress up the cake with lemon sorbet, or whipped cream. Or fresh berries and crème fraîche can be wickedly good. My mother has been known to garnish her store-bought cake with wild violets, her signature flower.

There is nothing like a scratch cake, especially if it was baked in the kitchen of a divine cook. It might be costly, but you don't have to wash a single dish. As my grandmother used to say: You find the best food at church. Serve the cake on a china plate and garnish with a daisy. Act mysterious when your guest holds out his plate and says, "More, please. And may I have the recipe?"

How to Make Key Lime Pie

Feed a man lemon pie if you want him to confess his secrets. Feed him brownies if you're in the mood for kissing. But beware of the key lime pie. It's the food of infidels. The lime juice goes straight from a man's mouth to his genitals.

—Aunt Tempe, explaining the connection between desserts and love to a broken-hearted woman, December 1992

The key lime pie is an evocative dessert, a renowned love enhancer. If you choose to make one, consider the main ingredient: north of Florida, there are no key lime trees. Gourmet groceries probably stock them, but in my small town, I am lucky to get Persian limes—those hard, green, egg-shaped fruits that proliferate all over the country. I have never tasted a fresh key lime, and I know my pies must suffer because of it. Instead, I use bottled juice. And there is a difference between traditional lime juice, the type found in the green squeeze bottles, and the creamy, tawny key lime juice.

I use a brand called Nellie and Joe's Key Lime Juice. It must be good, because I've seen it at the Winn-Dixie in Perdido Key, Florida. Somehow it found its way to my local Kroger. Now, whenever I shop, I always buy at least four bottles, just in case the store decides not to reorder. (They did this with bow-tie pasta—all of a sudden it vanished.) For a long time now, I've been stockpiling the juice in my dining room, although it puzzles my dinner guests. "What are those bottles doing on the sideboard?" they'll ask.

"I'm hoarding key lime juice," I explain.

Key lime pie requires a homemade graham cracker crust. For years I bought ready-made versions and thought nothing of it. A pie was a pie, a crust was a crust. Then I discovered how much I enjoyed the taste of buttery crumbs and the way I could mold them to fit any pie pan. Also, it was effortless. The day I made my first graham cracker crust was a turning point. I knew my store-bought days were over, knew I could trust my hands to shape something close to piecrust art. The crust takes about three minutes to prepare and will never fail you; or, as Mother says, "A good crust will never desert you." I don't know if she was talking about men or crusts. My mother believed that pies were meant to be divided—unlike a man. However, you certainly wouldn't want to eat a whole one at a single sitting.

Yield: 8 servings

PREPARATION FOR THE CRUST

  1 cup graham cracker crumbs

  ¼ cup sugar

  ½ stick unsalted butter, melted

  ⅔ cup blanched almonds, lightly toasted
    and cooled, then chopped

If you prefer a finer texture, use a food processor—bear in mind that texture creates mystery. Blend the ingredients, then shape into a buttered pie pan. Understand that the crust takes on the shape of the pan, and the filling assumes the shape of the crust, just as husbands mold wives and wives mold husbands. Bake at 350 degrees for 8 to 10 minutes. Cool. This crust is delicious with many fillings: cheesecake, lemon meringue, but it is particularly stunning with key lime. The nuts, which can't be found in a store-bought product, add complexity.

The soul of any pie is the filling, and the modern cook is faced with a dozen choices—there are hundreds of recipes for key lime pie. Perhaps it's the evocative name, or the old-timey way of adding green food color to the filling, but the key lime pie is a classic. It's the kissing cousin to the lemon meringue, that staple of roadside cafes, church socials, and picnics. Yet the key lime has an air of romance; it's the beautiful cousin who ran away to Europe and lives a glamorous life on a private Greek island.

Key lime pie is exotic, yet American, a medley of flavors and textures—sweet, sour, creamy, crunchy. It should be tart, sour yellow, but edged with sweetness. If it's green, you can be sure it's not genuine key lime. In most recipes the ingredients are similar: sweetened condensed milk, eggs, key lime juice, and, in some cases, extra sugar. The quantities are negotiable.

How to Prepare a Key Lime Filling

  3 large eggs, separated
  One 14-ounce can sweetened condensed milk
  ½ cup key lime juice
  Pinch of salt
  3 tablespoons tequila

Zest from 1 lime (the bright green Persians are fine)

Whipped cream, optional

In a large bowl, beat the yolks. Add the condensed milk. Stir in the lime juice, a little at a time. Add the salt and tequila. Stir till everything is blended. Add the zest. Spoon the filling into the shell. Chill one hour. Just before serving, whip the cream. Or, if you prefer a meringue, bring the egg whites to room temperature. In a large mixing bowl, beat the whites until stiff peaks form, adding a pinch of salt. Gradually add ⅓ cup sugar. Spread over the chilled filling. Bake 350 degrees, or until the meringue starts to brown. Chill, or eat right away. Garnish with zest and lime slices. This pie cries out for a supper on the porch—mango chicken, a roasted corn salad, and garlic bread. A full moon adds whimsy, but you can always string paper lanterns in the trees.

MORE INSTRUCTIONS

There's a certain whimsy to key lime pie. It's a favorite at trendy cafes and bakeries, where the desserts are displayed in round glass cases, with the sweets lined up on revolving shelves. Look but do not touch. Picture your husband eyeing a tart at his office (a place you rarely go). Your desserts have been traditional, and key lime is your most unconventional offering. Consider Eve and the apple. Like any paradise, Eden had its perils as well as its pleasures. People hunger for the forbidden. Look at Lot's wife. She just *had* to look back at the twin cities, and the next thing you knew, she was table salt.

Stolen pies are always sweeter when the heart pounds, when the gorging is clandestine. Even the most alluring dessert can become repellent if served with every meal. You long for apple cobbler, ambrosia, baked Alaska—anything that surprises the tongue. Imagine your husband in a locked glass case. You could take him out whenever you craved him. Eat your pie slowly, savoring each bite. Put the rest in the case, where it is safe, guarded, inviolate. If the glass becomes marred by fingerprints, wipe them away with a damp cloth. Understand that theft may occur when your back is turned, or right under your nose. Shake your head. Meditate on the tenacity of thieves. Tell yourself that nothing is inviolate. Ignore your mother when she says it takes two to tango, that the pie *wanted* to be stolen.

After you spend so much time making your pie, you hate to eat it. (Even failed pies are difficult to throw away.) You suspect that once you start slicing, you won't be able to stop; and then you will be left with nothing. You cannot have your pie and eat it, too. A pie won't last forever. Understand that eggs can spoil and meringue will weep. Consider the shelf life of love. Consider what would happen if marriages came stamped with expiration dates. Ponder your parents' marriage: forty-nine years of the same pie. If you hoard it, the filling will eventually sour and shrivel, pulling away from the crust. It will harden and crack, then finally disintegrate. Dust to dust, crumb to crumb. You will have no choice but to throw it out.

Read Faulkner's classic love story "A Rose for Emily." Imagine keeping a pie in your bedroom for a couple of decades. Something like that is bound to draw flies and vermin. Recall that the duchess of Windsor kept a slice of wedding cake from her third marriage—preserved in a white silk ribbon-tied box. Marvel when the slice brings £28,000 at Sotheby's. Realize that you don't want a marriage under glass. Honeymoons aren't feasts where the dessert is served first. Shrug. Tell yourself that man cannot live by pie alone. When people ask for the recipe, smile: It's been in your family a long time.

Always remember that the sweetest men bake *you* pies. (There is nothing more alluring than eating food that someone else has prepared just for you.) If you are the cook it helps to remember that a pie is served with your best intentions and your wildest dreams; but there is always risk. Some pies taste sour, others are falsely sweet. Understand that a pie consists of more than ingredients; it contains time, sacrifice, and a desire to please.

You must trust a recipe until it fails you. Unexpected events might occur: The humidity may rise and your meringue won't stiffen. You may drop the pie or smash it into someone's face. Food and violence are inexorably entwined—but so are food and love.

When you give a pie to someone, you cannot take it back; it's as unthinkable as taking back your heart. Your pie is composed of organic elements: eggs, sugar, cream. You cannot unmake a pie. Once joined, the ingredients will not separate. Ponder the force of that bond. You can smash it, trash it, give it to the dog, but you cannot separate the elements—eggs poured back in the shell, juice returned to the lime.

A wise cook knows a few things for certain: Always use the freshest ingredients. Guard against spoilage. Don't be afraid to substitute and tinker, and don't forget to garnish. China plates and silver forks can set a formal tone, but sometimes the best-tasting pies are eaten with your fingers. Never forget that it is very sensual to bring a whole pie to bed. Unlike love, the flavor of key lime will improve with chilling. Understand that a pie isn't a still life. Pies are made to be eaten. We cannot thrive without sustenance. Share your pie or hoard it. Eat it all by yourself, slice by slice, in large, greedy triangles. Eat with caution or eat with abandon—it's your choice.

Consuming Passions

In Praise of Mayonnaise

Life without Miracle Whip is like a marriage without romance.
Mayonnaise, like love, is a binding agent.

—Mimi Little, grandmother and creator of the mayonnaise
sandwich

In a world of food stars, mayonnaise is a supporting actor. It provides the backdrop for sandwiches, adds depth to guacamole, and is the secret ingredient in crab cakes. Store-bought mayonnaise has the consistency of sour cream, and homemade versions are rich and feisty; but many critics claim it isn't versatile. Imagine mayonnaise on a taco or baked potato—imagine it on smoked salmon!

I know people who adore sour cream and despise mayonnaise. They talk about sour cream as if it's the little black dress of food, a spreadable Grace Kelly. They scoff at mayonnaise, calling it a fat lady in sweatpants. If you ask me, sour cream is a bit player—an actor with a churlish attitude. Mayonnaise has a sweeter nature. Sour cream is a rich divorcée, a woman who donates her time and money to worthy functions; but mayonnaise is a flirt, and a bit of a hussy. It will turn on a hot day. It is not advisable to leave it alone for many hours. You'll be sorry if you do.

In truth, mayonnaise blends famously with its rival: sour cream. Acting as a binding agent, mayonnaise is also a taste enhancer. It is easygoing and cooperative—an unsung hero in the kitchen. And it holds its own in the versatility department. You can dress it up in chicken salad and serve it to club ladies; you can smear it on bread, add a slice of bologna, and serve it to a child; or you can spoon it in a pastry bag and swirl it over tomato aspic. Also, mayonnaise and potatoes have an undeniable affinity. I wouldn't go so far as to say they are star-crossed lovers, but there is a definite attraction.

Mayonnaise enthusiasts are passionate about their brands: Hellmann's (which is made by Best Foods on the West Coast), Duke's (sold in North Carolina), Blue Plate (my brand), or Miracle Whip. Once my mother conducted a taste test, placing a dollop of each mayonnaise in tiny paper soufflé cups. Hellmann's was the hands-down favorite. Some cooks add a little lemon juice to their favorite store-bought brand to mimic the tartness of homemade.

Dedicated cooks, along with snooty dilettantes, make their own mayonnaise, debating endlessly about the dangers of egg yolks and methods of pouring oil (a fine stream is recommended). I have prepared homemade mayonnaise once. Call me peculiar, but I was disappointed. It's a deceptively simple process. An old chemistry professor called it an emulsion, and he wrote his mother's recipe on the blackboard: egg yolks, oil, lemon juice, salt, dry mustard, and sugar. Cayenne was optional. My own recipe was similar, cribbed from one of Mama's cookbooks, and its failure can be blamed on inexperience and faulty technique—

it helps to make mayonnaise in a food processor, not with an ancient egg beater. I was saddened by the color (a sickly yellow) and consistency (mop water). I returned to Blue Plate and never looked back. It may be full of preservatives and low-budget oils, but it's delicious.

For mayonnaise devotees, there is heated debate about mayonnaise versus salad dressing. Supermarket shelves are packed with both varieties, including fat-free and "lite" versions. While I use mayonnaise as a binder, salad dressing is sweeter, making it instantly palatable for submarine sandwiches. It's the cousin who shows up at family reunions in a lacy dress, gloves, and a hair bow. Plain old mayonnaise is the aunt who plays the organ at church. She is dependable and consistent. You can count on her to bring an entire meal when a loved one dies.

If you love mayonnaise, sooner or later you will make egg salad. I have an ongoing search for the ultimate recipe. Egg salad is comfort food. It is ambrosial with or without lettuce, on wheat toast or plain white bread. Each bite cheers the soul and sets the world right, even if it's only for a half hour or so. My friend Peggy claimed her salad was the ultimate. It involved lots of paprika and Blue Plate mayonnaise. She offered to make it and dragged out a giant pan. After the eggs started boiling, she walked outside to pull weeds. A neighbor strolled over, and Peggy lost track of time. When she stepped into the kitchen, the pan had boiled dry, and it was making an odd popping noise. Shells were everywhere—on the counter, the floor, all over her cookbook shelf. She looked up: The eggs were even stuck to the ceiling.

"They just exploded," said Peggy, her pretty blue eyes widening. "Yolk and egg white in that immaculate kitchen. When I cleaned up, I broke down and cried."

I thought that was the funniest story I'd ever heard, until a few weeks later I myself detonated some eggs. I was heartsick, because those eggs were for Paul Shipley's famous egg salad, a recipe that deserves the James Beard award. It took me a long time to find this recipe—forty years of ceaseless hunting. I came upon the recipe in Arkansas at a potluck dinner. Paul Shipley, an avid reader and a distinguished Southern cook, had brought egg salad. When I went back for a second helping, the bowl had mysteriously vanished. Later, I found my husband in a corner, scraping the leftovers with a lettuce leaf. Paul was nice enough to give me the recipe.

Paul Shipley's Egg Salad
Yield: 4 to 6 servings

12 large eggs, hard-boiled
1 or 2 tablespoons finely chopped onion
10 pimiento-stuffed olives, chopped
2 small sweet pickles, finely chopped

1 tablespoon sweet pickle juice
Black pepper and salt to taste
Mayonnaise to bind (approximately 4 to 6 tablespoons)

Paul Shipley says, "Mix and enjoy and have your blood cholesterol checked regularly." Serve on any type of bread, but sourdough is especially tasty. This dish travels well to picnics, potlucks, and church socials.

Consuming Passions

I thought mayonnaise was a Southern condiment that had spread to the rest of the country, but I was wrong. Mayonnaise was created in France. I grew up thinking my grandmother had invented it. She served chicken salad to her sisters and the Eastern Star ladies. To this day I don't understand why Southern diners don't offer a mayonnaise sandwich on the menu. I always thought they were synonymous with a Southern childhood. But I could be wrong.

Last spring, I took an informal poll in North Carolina and was shocked to find a nest of mayonnaise haters. As they sang the virtues of mustard and vinaigrette, my heart sank. My own baby son is a mayonnaise hater, but I had hopes of converting him. I made a feeble attempt to proselytize to these women—all of them excellent cooks. I asked them if they'd ever eaten a chocolate mayonnaise cake. Yes, they admitted. Of course.

And if they were true mayonnaise haters, how did they make artichoke and spinach dips? How did they prepare salmon mousse? Another lady answered with a recipe. "Take a can of drained artichoke hearts, a cup of Duke's mayonnaise, and a cup of Parmesan. Blend in a food processor. Then bake in a shallow pan at three hundred and fifty degrees for thirty minutes. Serve with Triscuit crackers."

"Does it have to be Duke's?" I asked.

"Has to be," said the woman, lowering her eyebrows. A pit stop was made at the nearest Harris Teeter, and within minutes I was holding a jar of Duke's in my sweaty hands. Then, as we drove down the streets of Charlotte, one of the women asked if I could stand to live without sour cream. Yes, and I would grudgingly give up horseradish and cream cheese; but I couldn't imagine a world without mayonnaise. Bacon deviled eggs would cease to exist, along with my five favorite salads: chicken, potato, shrimp, lobster, and egg. I spouted off a mayonnaise litany: garlic, jalapeño, curry, pistachio, sesame, chipotle, orange, caper, dill, vegan.

One of the ladies said, "Me, I couldn't function socially without chicken salad—it *rules* at the ladies' clubs."

I rested my case.

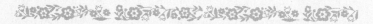

Tearoom Chicken Salad
Yield: 4 generous servings

3 pounds chicken breasts, simmered in seasoned water* for 15 minutes.**
½ cup roughly chopped celery
½ cup chopped onion
2 minced green onions
1 or 2 tablespoons fresh parsley, minced (optional)
½ cup mayonnaise, preferably Blue Plate, thinned with 1 teaspoon lemon juice
1 tablespoon lime juice (key lime is best)

2 tablespoons sour cream
1 tablespoon Dijon mustard
1 tablespoon honey
2 tablespoons white wine or champagne vinegar
Kosher salt and freshly ground pepper to taste
1 cup toasted pecans, chopped
1 cup sliced red (seedless) grapes (optional)
Extra parsley and grapes for garnish (optional)

*Have fun experimenting with "seasoned" water: Add to your pot a quartered onion, bits of red or green peppers, 4 stalks celery with leaves, carrots, fresh parsley (any amount), garlic, 1 teaspoon peppercorns, and 1 bay leaf.
**For the lazy or time-rushed, one or two deli-roasted chickens will suffice—remove the skin and cut up the white meat.

Consuming Passions

In a large bowl, mix the chicken, celery, onion, green onions, and the optional parsley. In a smaller bowl, blend the mayonnaise thinned with the lemon juice, lime juice, sour cream, mustard, honey, and vinegar. Mix well. Add salt and pepper to taste. Spoon the mayonnaise sauce over the chicken. Blend. Add pecans and grapes. Lightly blend. Serve in a nest of red Boston lettuce leaves; garnish with parsley and surround with melon slices, berries, and seedless grapes.

This salad can be served on the porch, as a sandwich for lunch, or piled onto red lettuce leaves for supper. Melon balls and a few scattered pecans add color and texture. Lemon icebox pie—with a graham cracker crust—is a traditional dessert.

When your heart is heavy, chicken salad won't work; it's too airy, too dainty. A melancholy soul requires substance—finger food that's profound, both in calories and comfort. The best cure in the world is a mayonnaise, bacon, and avocado sandwich, preferably accompanied by a large glass of sweet tea.

Make no mistake: This sandwich is composed of fat. It's not good for you, and I would never recommend eating it every day, unless you are as thin as linguine, with a cholesterol count of eighty. However, as my Mimi used to say, "One little sandwich won't kill you." Medically speaking, she was absolutely right—a rare indulgence can be healing. Once in a blue moon, when my spirit is gloomy, I always find myself in the kitchen making a bacon and avocado sandwich, slathering on mayonnaise and setting the world right.

Picking Grapes in August

When I eat grape jelly, it makes me think of good literature. The Grapes of Wrath, "Planet of the Grapes," and "The Grape Santini."

> —Aunt Dell, eating toast and jam at Bud and Lila's Cafe, 1992

You'll know it is time to harvest when the birds circle the vines and the air turns purple. Tie on a straw hat, one that belonged to your grandmother, and grab your child's red metal sand bucket. Then step into the garden. If you go early, you can see bumblebees diving into the clematis; but it is best to wait until mid-morning, when the snakes are sunning on the rocks. Just to be careful, beat the weeds with a stick.

As you step toward the grapes, your thoughts turn lilac; the sun presses against your shoulders like a firm hand. Reach into the leaves where it's at least ten degrees cooler, pinching off ripe clusters. You bite down on a grape; a burst of tart and sweet explodes on your tongue. This is not the time for greed. It is wise to let small grapes ripen; leave others for the birds. There's plenty to go around.

Your fingers work the vines, feeling where you cannot see. As the grapes fall into the pail, they ring against the metal. In minutes, the shiny red bottom disappears. Behind you, the cat stretches full length in the garden, his tail thumping against the vines. Blue jays caw from the trees, and the cat's ears swivel. When the pail is full and the handle cuts into your wrist, it is time to stop picking. Always remember that today's unripe grape will be tomorrow's prize, even if the birds peck it first. As you walk toward the house, the cat following at a discreet distance, you recite recipes in your mind.

Grape Jelly
Yield: 8 to 9 ½-pint jars

About 4 pounds grapes (to yield 4 cups grape juice)
7 cups sugar

One 3-ounce pouch liquid pectin

Sort, wash, and stem the grapes. Crush. Add ½ cup water and bring to a boil in a speckled enamel pan. Reduce heat and simmer for 10 minutes. Turn into a damp jelly bag. Drain well. Do not squeeze. Keep the juice overnight in a cool place, then strain through 2 thicknesses of damp cheesecloth. Measure four cups of juice into the kettle. Add the sugar. Mix well. Bring to a rolling boil. Add the pectin, and bring to another rolling boil. Let it boil hard for 1 minute. Remove the pan from the heat. Skim off the foam. Ladle the jelly into hot ½-pint jars. Leave a little headroom, about ¼ inch. Cap and screw on the bands—loosely. Process for 7 minutes in a hot-water bath. Cool upright.

Cocktail Franks in Grape Sauce
Yield: 4 to 6 servings

1 cup grape jelly
1 cup chili sauce
¼ teaspoon ground nutmeg
¼ teaspoon ground cinnamon
½ teaspoon ground ginger

1½ teaspoons soy sauce
4 teaspoons red wine
2 teaspoons mustard
Miniature cocktail franks or
    kielbasa slices

Mix together all the ingredients, except for the franks or sausage. Put in a crockpot or heavy saucepan and heat, stirring occasionally. When the jelly melts, add miniature cocktail franks or kielbasa slices. Sometimes I've added tiny, precooked meatballs. Cover; simmer 1 hour. Serve in a chafing dish.

Grapes are versatile. You can put them in chicken salad, sangria, or marinate them in brandy. If you aren't inclined toward cooking, or if your grapes taste sour, leave them for the birds. Train your vines to grow across a pergola. It takes a few seasons, but they can form a roof, like the one at Christina Campbell's tavern in Williamsburg. From spring through fall, you can eat outside while it's raining, and not a single drop will fall on your head.

When you gather grapes, it helps to remember that goddesses often lurk in the vines. Read *The Color Purple* and *Riders of the Purple Sage*. Plant delphiniums, irises, hyacinths, pansies, lavender, and Russian sage. If sour grapes are a problem in your life, add a pinch of sugar. Remind yourself that grapes are an ancient food, and a source of vitamin A. When they shrivel, they turn into iron-rich raisins. Read poetry—"When I Am an Old Woman I Shall Wear Purple." As you bite into a grape, close your eyes and let your thoughts bloom like wild violets.

How to Make Sugared Violets

When cooked, violet leaves become stringy, the same way okra does. In a pinch, use minced violets to thicken your gumbo. Add generous tweaks to the food of your beloved to induce sleep and dispel anger.

—From the papers of Mama Hughes, notes scribbled on the back of a seed packet, 1928

Yield: Approximately 50 violets

PREPARATION

    50 violets (plus a few extra, as some

      specimens will not survive)

    2 egg whites

    1 cup sugar

Make certain your flowers, like your sweetheart, have been grown organically. Avoid all violets that have been sprayed with chemicals or bottled fertilizers; the aftereffects are insidious, and, in some cases, fatal. A coddled garden is sometimes the worst place of all. Be suspicious if you don't see any weeds. Wild violets, while alluring, have unknown histories. As with mushrooms, it is best to exercise caution. Find edible flowers from a gardener you trust—or better yet, grow your own. If that is not possible, peruse the gardener's shed, looking for herbicides and other poisons. If you even suspect the slightest contamination, discard the flowers and find another source.

For the sake of cleanliness, your violets must be washed. Prepare two bowls of water. In the first bowl, add four drops of Joy liquid, then swish the water until a few bubbles form. Cautiously lift the violet and dip it into the soapy mixture; use the second bowl for rinsing. In assembly-line fashion, continue cleaning and rinsing the violets. Dry on paper towels.

Beat the egg whites until foamy. Holding a violet by its stem, dip it into the egg. Over a shallow bowl, spoon the sugar over the damp violet. Dipping is not recommended. This is a turbulent procedure, and many of your specimens will perish if great care is not taken. In this respect, the sugaring of violets is very much like sugaring a man—a delicate touch is encouraged.

Set the survivors on a baking sheet. The flowers are at their weakest, and many of them will look a little careworn; now is the time to reshape them with a sewing needle, cautiously arranging the petals into an appealing shape. Some of the flowers will disintegrate, but that is why you have extras. Fingernail clippers are a useful tool for deftly snapping off the stems.

Bake the violets at 150 degrees for 5 minutes. Turn off the oven and let the blossoms sit in the oven overnight. The next day, gently transfer the violets to a long, shallow plastic container. Airtight is best. Refrigeration is not necessary as long as you store them in a cool place.

Remember that violets are symbolic of romance, and also of reliability. Napoleon never forgot to bring a bouquet to Josephine, and Zeus himself was credited with creating the purple flower. He was having a fling with a nymphet, Io, and in order to hide her from his jealous wife, he changed the nymph into a cow. Zeus thought he would have his cake and eat it, too, but Io found the situation dreadful. The grass was bitter and unpalatable—before Io became a heifer, she'd dined on nectar of the gods. Now, she began to weep, and Zeus, looking down on his mistress, changed her tears into violets. Whether or not he turned her back into a woman remains unclear.

Now that your petals have been crystallized, they are everlasting, like your love is supposed to be but with one amazing difference: The violets are edible.

Gumbo Ya-Ya

A Pot of Gumbo

Elderly Creole ladies were fond of gathering at each other's houses to spend the day. All the gossip would be exchanged, family histories combed through, the actions of this person or that discussed. Dreading exposure to the night air, the ladies would scurry home just before dusk, well supplied with gossip for a long time to come. . . . Such a gathering of women was known, scornfully, as a gumbo ya-ya.

—From *Gumbo Ya-Ya: A Collection of Louisiana Folk Tales*
(Gretna: Pelican Publishing Company, 1988)

My mama is a sweet, Southern lady; but if you want to make her mad, just brag about someone else's cooking. One Thanksgiving, the whole family drove down to Perdido Key, Florida, to stay in a borrowed condominium on the bay. My father bought a metal crab trap and filled it with chicken necks. Every morning, when he pulled the trap from the water, it was full of crabs.

"We're gonna have good gumbo," he said.

One morning Mama and the other relatives drove to the outlet mall. "Are you *sure* you don't want to go?" Mama asked me. I shook my head. I wanted to hang around the kitchen and help my father boil crabs—an essential ingredient for our gumbo. I could not remember a holiday that did not feature this soup.

Mama excelled in making all kinds of gumbo, but she loathed the messier side of preparation. And it is a daunting concoction, even for seasoned cooks. Duck gumbo is a painstaking procedure, separating the precious meat from delicate bones, along with the disposal of an enormous amount of feathers. It requires nimble fingers and a settled stomach. It is a luxurious broth, yet wholly different from its cousin, seafood gumbo. In this soup, the oysters must be coaxed from impenetrable shells, and dozens of raw shrimp must be peeled and deveined. If you are lucky enough to live near the ocean, fresh crabmeat lends an ambrosial touch to gumbo. Bear in mind that live crabs can make you pine for a whole separate kitchen for boiling, cracking, and picking the luscious meat. It is a smelly and boring operation, one of those thankless culinary tasks that always fall to the rookie chef.

In this borrowed Florida kitchen, this task fell willingly to me and my father. We hated to shop. Mama, on the other hand, despised picking crabmeat. "I'd just as soon peel grapes with my teeth," she always said.

In a bottom cabinet, Daddy and I found a huge pot. We filled it with water, beer, Zatarain's crab boil, extra bay leaves, and Tabasco. When the crabs were done, we let them cool a bit, then we picked them on the kitchen table, over thick layers of the *Mobile Register*. I liked watching my father's hands move over the crabs, finding white meat in obscure places. It was tedious work, but if you wanted excellent gumbo, it was necessary. Sometimes he'd whistle old songs from World War II, and I'd try to guess the titles. The whole time, his hands never stopped moving. In our house, fresh crabmeat was as precious as caviar. Nothing was wasted. I wasn't adept at crab picking, so I used an old fondue fork to reach into the crevices. "It's like mining," Daddy said. "Mining for great gumbo."

When the last claw was cracked, we decided to go fishing—our reward for doing Mama's dirty work. We packed up our gear, threw on hooded sweatshirts, and walked across the highway, over to the beach. When I was a tiny girl, my father would strap me in an orange life vest, set me between his legs, and launch his boat into a bayou. He said I could fish as well as any boy. Over the years, we'd caught amberjack, red snapper, even a few sharks. Once, off the coast of Daytona Beach, we snagged a baby octopus, which we quickly tossed back into the Atlantic. In Panama City we caught a blue crab on the beach. It was a she-crab, packed with eggs, and Daddy made us let her go. She scurried into the water as fast as she could, floating for a long time before she disappeared.

Now, standing on the windy beach, we rigged up the poles and began casting into the cold Gulf of Mexico. It was a winter ocean, the color of dishwater, and each big wave left tiny bubbles on the sand. Whenever I am fishing, I lose track of everything; time and troubles fall away. I felt a tug on the line and I jerked the pole, trying to set the hook, but it was useless. These Panhandle fish were cunning. A blue heron stood at a discreet distance, watching our bait with interest. My daddy threw him a morsel, and the heron gratefully snapped it up. "I doubt we'll catch anything," Daddy said, gazing up at the clouds. "I don't like how the sky looks."

"What's wrong with it?" I looked up. I didn't see anything but clouds and a few pelicans.

"It's not a fishing sky," he said. "But we'll see. Maybe we'll get lucky."

"If we catch something, Mama can put it in the gumbo," I teased. One thing about my mother—she'd cook anything we brought home, any time of day or night. As long as you didn't ask her to pick crabs or shuck oysters, she'd happily grill a flounder, stuffing it full of herbs and bacon, or she'd fry catfish that melted on the tongue.

"Sheesh," said Daddy. "She'd never put fish in her gumbo. Or okra."

We fished until our arms gave out. Daddy's prophesy was correct: We didn't catch a thing, but it didn't matter. I loved the rituals of fishing—reeling, casting, fiddling with lures, untangling the lines. Daddy always said that fishing taught a child patience. You could cast into an ocean all day long, combining your best ability with your best intentions, and it was still possible to come up empty-handed. But it didn't necessarily mean you'd wasted your time.

❧ ☙

The next day brought another carload of relatives, and if you listened hard, you could keep track of ten conversations going on at the same time. Meanwhile, Mama baked an enormous turkey. She also fixed the gumbo, using our crabmeat, along with a pot of rice. Aunt Joyce helped with the oyster dressing; the cousins made sweet potato casserole and ambrosia. A sister-in-law brought pies from the beach bakery. Aunt Dell showed up with a coconut cake, and one wedge was missing. I made yeast rolls.

"When's that gumbo going to be ready, Ary Jean?" somebody asked.

Gumbo Ya-Ya

Mama stood by the pot, protecting it with a giant spoon. "Not till I *say* so," she warned. A word about Mama and her gumbo. She's a little evangelical on the subject. She believes there is one way to make gumbo: *her* way. All other methods and recipes are not only wrong but inferior. She thinks the addition of okra is a grievous faux pas. Her gumbo is rusty brown, full of oysters, shrimp, and crabmeat. Each spoonful brings up bits of celery, chips of onion. The broth seems to quiver, like fireworks. When you swallow, little sparks fly down your throat, but the explosion occurs in the brain.

The day after Thanksgiving, my daddy got it in his head to have dinner at the Pensacola Officers' Club; they were supposed to have a fabulous Friday night buffet. "But we're not in the navy," said Mama. "They'll throw us out."

"I think it's open to the public," said Daddy.

"You *think*," she scoffed.

On Friday evening, the atmosphere was festive. Mama dressed up in a red caftan. Daddy passed a bottle of champagne. My sister-in-law poufed up everybody's hair, then she sat down in the middle of the floor and painted her nails Tabasco red. My youngest child sat at the table, working a puzzle and humming. Finally, Aunt Dell appeared in something that resembled black draperies.

"Let's go," said Mama. We squeezed into three cars and drove to the naval base. From the radio, Bing Crosby was singing "White Christmas," and we'd had just enough champagne to sing along. At the base, a guard stopped us, then flicked on a flashlight, sweeping the beam into the car. "We're on our way to the buffet," said my daddy, holding up his driver's license. Our sheer numbers must have scared the man, because he stepped back and waved us through.

The officers' club was a handsome white building, hidden by live oaks and imported palms. The St. Augustine grass was roped off with chains—"Typical military," said Mama. Music drifted out onto the lawn. We stepped past a bar that was full of good-looking pilots in bomber jackets. They all gawked at Dell, who seemed to float in her black ensemble. Mama strode ahead, swinging an enormous canvas pocketbook.

In the dining room, the waitress took one look at us and hastily jammed two long tables together. The room had high ceilings, illuminated by tiered brass chandeliers. Most of the diners were officers and their families. We lined up at the buffet. Mama nodded to a naval wife, who was loading a plate with macaroni salad. My mother liked to make friends with strangers. When my brother and I were small, she would embarrass us in grocery stores by striking up conversations with the other shoppers. And she can't travel on a plane without becoming pals with everyone on board. The naval wife drifted off, and Mama turned her attention to two children who were eating whipped cream straight from the dessert bar. They took turns licking the spoon, and when they were through, they put it back into the whipped cream.

Everyone dipped up a bowl of gumbo—except Mama. "It's got okra in it," she hissed. "They don't know how to cook in Florida." But the navy gumbo was delicious. My husband and sister-in-law went back for seconds. Dell loudly scraped her spoon against the bowl. Even my daddy, who was raised over in Biloxi, stood in line for another serving.

"How can you eat that?" Mama said, rolling her eyes. "Only yesterday I served the very *finest* gumbo. It was loaded with crab-meat."

"But it's good," I said, holding out my cup. A tiny crab claw floated in the bottom. "Want a taste?"

"I do *not*," she snapped; but she peered into my bowl. "It's orange."

"It's the best gumbo I've ever eaten," said my husband, fitting the spoon into his mouth. Dell snorted. Everyone at the table stopped talking, looking from Mama to my husband. A wisp of steam drifted from her ears.

"What did you say?" Mama's voice was cold.

"Taste it for yourself, Ary Jean," said my husband.

"It really is good, Nanny," said my baby son.

"It's just like my mama used to make," said Daddy.

"Get you a bowl," said my brother.

"Get the recipe," said my sister-in-law.

"IT'S GOT OKRA!" Mama cried.

"I've never heard of a gumbo recipe without okra or filé," I said.

"Don't ask me," said Dell, holding up her hands. "For years I thought gumbo was a voodoo curse."

"Okra and filé are trash! I've had it!" Mama slapped her napkin against the table. A few officers turned around to stare. "If one more person mentions this gumbo," she said, "I'm going to climb up on this table and swing from the chandelier."

"And she will," said my daddy, lowering his eyebrows. Two things will make my mama crazy—if you hurt her children or belittle her cooking. Then she'll get a little wild.

"Gumbo!" said my baby son, thinking this was a game. Everyone stopped breathing. Mama pushed back her chair and hiked up her red caftan, ready to crawl on the table, but my daddy grabbed her arm.

"Sit down, honey," he said. "Please. People are staring."

"I don't care what they think." Mama lifted her chin.

"Be nice," warned Daddy. "Please."

"All right," said Mama. "But if I hear the word 'gumbo,' if I even hear the *guh* sound, then I'm grabbing that chandelier. Understood?"

We all nodded. Just then our waitress appeared. She eyed our empty soup bowls. "Isn't the gumbo great?" she said.

Mama was fast, a blur in a red caftan. She grabbed the chandelier's brass arm and started swinging.

A Letter from Mama

Dear Michael Lee,

Here is the gumbo recipe you wanted. We had it to-nite and ate a pot-ful with Jimmy. I didn't have fresh crabs, but it was delicious. Poor Jimmy was at loose ends. A $200,000 machine broke today because some-one at the plant was careless and didn't add oil. It took gumbo and rice and beer to calm him, and even that really didn't help. He is heartsick that someone tore up his machine. I would feel the same way if someone messed with my gumbo. Here is my recipe. Guard it.

Gumbo Ya-Ya

Ary Jean's Gumbo
Enough to fill a 4-quart pot

CHOP
3 onions
3 stalks celery
1 medium green bell pepper
4 green onions
3 cloves garlic, minced, not
    chopped
1 tablespoon chopped fresh
    parsley

Salt and pepper to taste

GET READY
1 pound peeled, deveined
    shrimp
1 can crabmeat
1 pint fresh oysters

MAKE A ROUX

Over medium flame, heat ½ cup olive oil, then whisk in ½ cup all-purpose flour. You have to whisk (some cooks stir) over medium heat and you can't leave it until it's the color of an old copper penny. This is the secret to your gumbo, and its heart. If you burn it, start over. Be sure it's really brown or your gumbo will look gray. Filé powder or okra is for sissy cooks; a well-made gumbo needs no outside thickening agents. It all starts with the roux, and mine is superior to all others.

Now sauté your vegetables in olive oil. Add the chopped fresh parsley. Add to the pot 4 quarts boiling water, 1 tablespoon salt, and lots of black pepper. Cook about 4 hours, covered. Now you are ready to add your seafood. Add it and boil vigorously for about 8 minutes. Reduce the heat and simmer. While the gumbo cooks, make your rice. Eat to your heart's content. To prepare a larger batch, you have to increase the amount of roux accordingly. I served this with a Caesar salad and fresh bread. Wish you were here because it was the best gumbo I've ever made.

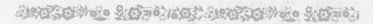

Love,

Your Mama

Raw

Don't talk to me about diets. All men like women with bubble butts.

> —Aunt Dell, arguing with her sister Lula, standing outside
> Jenny Craig, Dijon, Louisiana, 1989

Aunt Lula taught aerobics at a health club, and one Christmas she gave Dell a guest pass. "You can do step-fit, water aerobics, or yoga," Lula said. "And our gym has state-of-the-art machines."

"I hate to sweat," said Dell. She knew all about exercise. Step-fit was a brutal form of exertion that involved jumping up and down and over a set of horrid plastic steps. This activity caused the pulse rate, as well as the appetite, to race out of control. Dell personally believed she could *save* calories by staying home with a bag of marshmallows and watching reruns of *Twilight Zone.*

"Sweating is good for you. Just one visit," Lula promised, "and you'll be hooked. Exercise is addictive."

"So is tobacco," snapped Dell.

"It makes a woman glow," said Lula.

"Cigarettes do that?" Dell drew back, her forehead wrinkled.

"Don't tease me." Lula pursed her pouty little lips. "Exercise lowers the cholesterol."

"I don't want to be a muscle woman," Dell said, giving her sister a skeptical gaze.

"You'll drop a dress size."

"Sure I will," said Dell, bursting open a bag of Fritos.

"Look, I've even gotten you some outfits." Lula handed Dell a stack of cotton T-shirts. "I culled them from my closet."

"Will these fit me?" Dell lifted a shirt that said PANAMA CITY, FLORIDA. Beneath the letters, two airbrushed divers were locked in a provocative position; their bubbles rose to the surface, where BUD'S DIVE SHOP was spelled out in red letters.

"They'll fit," said Lula.

"You're fifteen sizes smaller than me," said Dell.

"They're from my exes," said Lula, reaching into the collar, turning the label inside out. "See? 'X-tra Large.' I've been cleaning closets."

"Which ex?" Dell smiled. "The sumo wrestler?"

"No, the lawyer," said Lula. "You never know who you'll meet at a gym."

That made sense to Dell. She dashed into Lula's bathroom and dressed in a hurry, pulling on gray cotton shorts. She held up a white shirt. On the pocket it said:

HALF SHELL

RAW BAR

KEY WEST

She hastily glanced at the back. There was more writing, but what caught Dell's attention was the art: a gorgeous, black-headed 1940s pinup girl smiled back at Dell. She wore high heels and lots of mascara. In one hand she held up a platter of raw oysters. Dell herself had once been a looker. Not skin and bones like the girls of today, but a woman of circumference, not to mention her own natural-born cleavage. It was too bad that the cartoon woman was festooned on the back of the shirt, where Dell couldn't admire it while she worked out. She hoped everybody thought she'd bought the shirt in Key West—a world traveler she wasn't, but she liked to create a glamorous image.

She pulled the shirt over her head. Then she drove to the gym. She halfway hoped the parking lot was full. Then she'd have an excuse to drive off. Even with the baggy shirt, she felt conspicuous. As luck would have it, the lot was empty except for three compact cars, the preferred type for aerobicized women. Inside the gym, a bouncy teenage trainer showed Dell how to work the treadmill and the weight machines. "Am I doing this right?" Dell kept asking.

"Perfect," said the little trainer, flipping her blond ponytail. She smiled. "You're doing fantastic."

"Do I look fat?" Dell hiked up her gray shorts. The cellulite began at her ankles, worsened at the knees, then grew into potholes on the backs of her thighs. "Tell me the truth."

"You look great," said the trainer. "And you'll look better every day."

"Me?" Dell looked in the mirror and squinted. "But I weigh over two hundred pounds."

"But you carry it well," said the trainer. "If you work out a minimum of three days a week, you'll have *the* most wonderful body."

"How many weeks?" said Dell.

"The body responds immediately to weight training," said the trainer.

"My sister works here," said Dell. "You know Lula?"

"Oh, wow. Do I ever." The trainer's eyes widened. "She's got a body that's, like, to die for."

"I used to have a body like that."

"And you will again," said the blonde.

Puffed up by the praise, Dell walked one mile on the treadmill. Then she slogged downstairs, sticking her head in the free-weight room. A bald-headed man was lifting free weights, making guttural sounds. And a blond, bearded man was sitting on a bench, doing wrist curls. When they saw Dell, they did a double take. Even with the hereditary cellulite, Dell thought to herself, men still stared. Flattered by the attention, she eased over to the water fountain, taking a dainty sip. Then she walked around, swinging her arms. The bald-headed man strode over to the water fountain and stared at her.

"Eat it raw?" he said. Dell felt a blush start at her ears, and she whirled around. In the wall-to-wall mirrors, she could see the man watching her. When she'd had a decent figure (38–24–39), men had often followed her down the street. Now, she turned and faced the bald-headed man. If he asked her to dinner and a movie, she'd go. But the little trainer bounced up, ruining everything.

"Since Lula works here," she told Dell, "I can give you a discount membership."

"Oh, I don't know," said Dell. The bald man was still staring.

"But you already look better," said the trainer, and Dell could have slapped her. "Remember, exercise is a privilege, not a chore."

On the way home, Dell stopped at Wal-Mart, loading her cart with jelly beans and Twizzlers—her favorite fat-free items. Behind her she heard whistling. She turned. Two hairy men were blowing kisses. "Damn," said the short one, "you're big, but I'd still eat you raw."

"Mmm-*mmm*," said the bigger man. He stuck out his tongue, licking the air.

Dell whirled around. What the *blank* was going on? First, she'd gotten stared down at the health club; now she was being harassed at Wal-Mart. She pushed the cart around the corner and rattled down another aisle. She could hear the perverts behind her, hooting and whistling. Narrowing her eyes, she glanced over her shoulder. The short man grinned, showing a row of dirty teeth. Then he reached for his crotch. "My van is parked just outside," he said. "Come on, baby. Show me a good ol' raw time."

"Get out of my way," Dell growled. She whirled around, dragging the cart, narrowly missing the short man. He hopped out of the way. "Feisty, ain't you?" he said.

"Stop bothering me!" Dell screeched.

"You asked for it, lady," said the tall pervert.

"I did not!" Dell looked around wildly, hoping another shopper would rescue her. She picked up a can of cashews and held it over her head. "Step back or I'll hit you in the head!"

       Gumbo Ya-Ya

"Whoa!" said the short pervert.

"Stalking is against the law," she yelled. "I'm calling the police."

"Fine, lady." The short pervert held up both hands. "But you'll have some explaining to do."

"Shut up!" Dell shook the cashew can. "I'll hit you between the eyes. I mean it!"

"If you didn't want no attention," said the little man, "then you shouldn't of wore that T-shirt."

"Leave my clothes out of this!" Dell eyed the men. As far as perverts went, they looked harmless. Just two old geezers shopping for ammunition and Bowie knives. After all, Louisiana was Sportsman's Paradise. But she had no intention of being their prey. She took a step closer, shaking the can again.

"She won't dare," said the short pervert. (He seemed to be in charge.)

Dell threw the can. It crashed into a vanilla wafer display. The men broke into a run. "You *blanks!*" she yelled. "*Blankety, blank blanks!*"

Dell marched out of the store, then drove over to her mother's house. "First, I went to the gym, and a bald-headed man eyeballed me," Dell told Tempe, opening a box of Whitman chocolates, ruffling through the papers. "Then two men stalked me at Wal-Mart. They whistled. And they tried to lick me. They almost tried to lure me into their vehicle."

"No wonder," Tempe said. "Look at your T-shirt."

"This?" Dell snatched a handful of fabric. "Lula gave it to me."

"Well, she shouldn't have," said Mama. "The shirt's a little suggestive."

"It's extra large!"

"Honey, it's not the size of the shirt, it's what's on it." Tempe reached for a chocolate.

"What, that silly woman on the back? She's not even naked."

"She doesn't have to be, Dell," said Tempe, laughing. "Eat It Raw."

"Eat what raw?" Dell eyed a chocolate, trying to decide if it was caramel, then popped it in her mouth.

"That's what the shirt says."

"It does?" Dell glanced over her shoulder, twisting her neck. Her lips moved as if she were whispering a secret to herself.

"Told you," said Tempe. "But look at it this way, at least your admirers can read."

"It's not the shirt," said Dell, leaning toward her mama. She lowered her voice. "It's my bubble butt."

"Then you need to keep it big," said Tempe. She held out the candy box. "Another chocolate, Dell?"

Kitchen Fires

Some women are just prone to grease fires. They attract them the way other gals attract men. Both types eventually go up in smoke.

—Aunt Dell, chocolate connoisseur and crazy woman, talking to an insurance adjuster, 1990

One March, I ran away from home. I ended up at Mama's, watching *Rebecca* in the king-size bed. Her prized bobtail cat, Tojo, lay between us, his ears flicking. "Mrs. Danvers needs a bottle of Nair," snorted Mama. She opened a box of Russell Stover chocolates, her fingers rustling the pleated papers.

"She *is* hairy," I admitted.

"Look at that low hairline. She needs a good beautician," Mama said.

"We shouldn't pick on Danvers," I said. "Anyway, the last time we saw *Rebecca*, you were against the new wife. You called her spineless."

"She is," said Mama. "And way too young for de Winter. I can see why Rebecca did what she did. But Danvers looks particularly bad tonight."

"Maybe it's your TV set," I said, yawning. I was trying to stay awake until Danvers went up in flames, but my eyelids kept shutting. I've learned to never make conversation with my mama just for the heck of it. She'll take up the gauntlet and talk your ears off. Above all, don't get her talking about food. She'll tell you what she had for supper and what her neighbors had for supper, and she'll even speculate on what distant kin are eating.

Just when I started to doze off for the tenth time, I thought I smelled smoke. I sat up in bed and drew in a deep breath. The cat sat up, too, his pupils dilating. There it was again, a burnt-rubber smell. I looked at Mama, and she looked at me. "What?" she said. We'd had French onion soup for supper, made from Vidalia onions. Mama was a superb cook, but she didn't believe in things like fire alarms, or any sort of alarm that might get her excited and raise her blood pressure.

"Did you leave the stove on?" I asked.

"I'd never do such a thing," she snorted. Then she rose up out of bed. "Well, I have. But not recently."

"Smell that?" I threw back the covers, and the cat sprang off the bed, racing down the hall. "Something's on fire."

Mama sat up, her eyes wide. I was already on my feet, running down the hall. In the little yellow kitchen, smoke was pouring from the ceiling. Mama took one look at it and jabbed me with her elbow. "See?" she cried. "It's the chandelier! I told you I didn't leave the stove on!"

"It must've shorted." I ran to the phone and called 911. Smoke poured out of the chandelier; it crackled twice, sending out sparks. A black stain was spreading across the white ceiling. It moved in a crinkly wave, the way paper burns. I grabbed my shoes, yelling for Mama to get out of the house.

"Where's my yellow caftan?" she muttered, digging through a pile of dresses.

"I just called 911," I said, pulling her arm. "The fireman said to get out."

"First, call your brother," Mama warned. When my brother Jimmy left home, he didn't move very far—he took up residence in the backyard. While I dialed his number, Mama pulled on a quilted housecoat, then she laced up Nike high-top sneakers.

"'Lo?" said Jimmy.

"The house is on fire," I said, trying to sound calm. Then, without further explanation, I slammed down the receiver.

"You're awful blunt tonight," Mama said.

"Hurry," I said, herding her toward the door. I scooped up pocketbooks and sweaters, and we rushed through the dining room. The table was set with violet-sprigged china and Francis 1ST sterling and purple thumbprint goblets. For as long as I could remember, she'd always set the table for breakfast the night before. Mama believed there was no point in having pretty things if you didn't use them. Now she didn't even glance at the table. We scurried out the door, angling down the porch steps, into the chilly March night.

As we stood in the driveway, stamping our feet against the cold, we heard the sirens. Red and blue lights swept down Algood Highway. Down in the culvert, we saw a long red truck speed up a hill, then curve dramatically in front of the house. Three other fire trucks were racing down the highway, tailed by an ambulance. My brother paced in the grass, his fingers jammed under his armpits. Up and down the road, the neighbors were waking up. Lights blazed from windows, and a few people opened their front doors and peeked out. This was an old, settled neighborhood, and most all the residents took digitalis to slow their fluttery hearts. I looked back at Mama, but she was talking to a fireman. She has a tendency to get wild when she is frightened; there was no telling what she would say or do. Right now she was telling the man about her onion soup. "And it didn't start this fire," she said, turning to glare at me.

"What's happened?" he asked.

"Ary Jean's house is on fire," said a neighbor.

The firemen were dressed like astronauts; in single file, they grimly marched into the house. "Just like in *Alien*," whispered Jimmy. "Cool!"

Five minutes later, the men reported that the fire was out—the chandelier had apparently shorted. "Bad wiring," he said.

"The ceiling is still real hot," said another. "We're going to stick around till it cools off."

Meanwhile, another neighbor, a widow with gray hair and bowed legs, brought up a tray—Styrofoam cups full of strong coffee. She kept apologizing for not having any doughnuts. One of the men let my brother sit in the police car and turn on the blue lights. Everybody kept saying how lucky Mama had been; it was a small fire, and no real damage was done. The most she'd have to do was replace the chandelier and paint the ceiling.

"Your daughter saved the day," said a fireman with a handlebar moustache. "I hate to think what would've happened if you-all had been asleep. You could've died, all of you."

"That's right," I said. "From smoke inhalation." I turned to Mama. She stared straight ahead, but her eyes looked glazed. I touched my fingertips to her wrist; her pulse was weak and thready.

"Maybe the paramedic should check you," I said, but she waved me off. I glanced around for my brother, but he was in the police car, pressing switches and gadgets. On top of the car, the blue lights merrily twirled.

"I'm fine," Mama said, running her hands through her short, wiry hair.

"You don't look fine, lady," said the mustached fireman.

Mama turned, her face crumpled. "Oh, *no!*" she cried.

"I didn't mean it the way it sounded," said the fireman, blushing. "You look all right. In fact, you look good, considering."

"Forget about me," Mama said, her voice rising. "I don't care about me! WHERE IS MY CAT?"

"Cat?" said the fireman, scrunching up his forehead. "I didn't see no cat."

"Poor little Tojo," Mama cried, clasping both hands under her chin. All of the screen doors were propped open with brooms. "I plain forgot about him. He's probably had a complete nervous breakdown by now."

"It'll come back," said the fireman.

"You don't know my cat." Mama began walking around the yard, peering under bushes, trying to lure Tojo with promises of canned crabmeat, his hands-down favorite. "Pus-*sy?*" she called. "Puss, puss, puss!"

"Damn," said the paramedic. "She feeds her cat crabmeat?"

"I could tell you plenty," said the gray-haired neighbor, raising her eyebrows. She held out the tray. "More coffee, anybody?"

"I'll just bet he ran out of the house and climbed a tree," Mama told the fireman. "That's how I found him. He was a runaway, and a dog treed him? For three days, I tried to coax him down, but he wouldn't budge." She pointed to an oak tree. "See? It was that tree over there. I had to call the fire department. Y'all got him down in a heartbeat. Well, not you, but one of your colleagues?" Mama had a tendency to let her voice rise at the end of a sentence, as if she was asking a question. This is her way of holding your interest.

All the firemen gazed up at the oak.

"I just know he's in bad trouble." Mama sighed.

"Don't worry, lady," said one of the firemen, "if he's treed, we'll get him down."

"Are you sure?" My mama looked up into his eyes.

"Sure I'm sure," he said, pulling off his helmet and slicking back his hair. "You never see any cat skeletons hanging from trees, do you?"

Several minutes later, a fireman spotted a cat on the roof. A ladder was summoned, and Tojo was coaxed down. "You saved my pussy," said Mama, gathering the cat into her arms.

The fireman looked stunned. "Excuse me, ma'am?"

"My cat," Mama said, rubbing Tojo's silver fur. "What else?"

"I wouldn't sleep here tonight," said another fireman, walking up.

"Why indeed not?" Mama looked indignant.

"Fumes," said the fireman.

"I refuse to abandon my house," Mama said.

"Mama," I said, "does the phrase 'carbon monoxide poisoning' mean anything to you?"

"Don't get sassy," she warned. "I'll just crack open a few windows and we'll be fine."

"We?" I blinked. "I'm not staying here."

"Thanks for the coffee, ma'am," said the fireman, walking backward, tipping his hat to me and Mama. "I swear, this was the nicest fire you ever had. I've been here before, six months ago? That grease fire?"

"Why, *yes!*" Mama clasped her hands under her chin. "I *do* remember."

"And a time before that, you burnt up a roast."

"I was garage-saleing that day. I let the roast simmer. It was a nice eye of round, too." Mama shook her head. "I'll never do that again."

The fireman nodded. "And another time, you burnt up a—"

"That's enough," warned Mama. "I get your drift."

"I'm not staying here," I said, gazing at the windows. A plume of smoke drifted out. "Those fumes are deadly."

"They sure are," said the fireman.

"Leave, then," said Mama. "I'm not afraid. I've been around smoke before, and I'm just fine. The cat will keep me company. He's almost human. Aren't you, Tojo?"

❧ ❦

Reader, I stayed. By the time we'd opened all the windows and turned on the television, the tail end of *Rebecca* was on. "They never show Manderley's kitchen," said Mama, stroking the cat.

"It wasn't a real house," I said. "There is no Manderley."

"I guess not," she said. "But I'll bet it had a gigantic kitchen. With miles of bad wiring."

"I can still smell smoke," I said.

"Then stick your nose under the covers, dear." Mama sighed. "You can never tell about crazy women and old wires. They'll snap and burn every time."

"Shh, Mama," I said, pointing to the TV. Danvers was standing in the window, ready to leap into the flames. "There she is."

"I'll bet she left the stove on," said Mama.

Under the Fig Leaf

Forget about looking at hands and feet. You can tell a real man by the size of his fig leaf.

—Tourist at Manci's Antique Club, July 1996

Mama and I were driving along Mobile Bay, searching for a place called Manci's Antique Club. It was reputed to have the biggest collection of Jim Beam decanters in the South, possibly the world. Mama has a thing about old liquor bottles. Her interest was sparked by my brother's childhood passion for empty decanters. When he was barely out of diapers, he would slog along the highway with a sack, pawing through trash cans. Then he'd drag home the booty. Mama would wash out the bottles and stack them in a row on his bedroom windowsill.

Now I glanced at her and said, "What time does this store close?"

"Two A.M.," she said.

"That doesn't sound right." I narrowed my eyes. "What kind of junk shop stays open that late?"

"This is no junk store. It's an antiques club," she said firmly, "not a regular antiques shop. And it most definitely stays open till two A.M. Trust me."

"Is this an auction house?" I gave her a swift, suspicious glance.

"Stop asking so many questions and drive," she said, arching one gray eyebrow. Mama doesn't fool me; bargain hunting is in her genes. She especially likes auctions in obscure towns, where Fiesta goes dirt cheap and sterling-silver forks turn up in dusty boxes. I spent my childhood in pawnshops where shifty-eyed owners panicked every time a police car drove by. The owners ran around the store, yanking down the window shades. Now, watching a sly smile spread across Mama's face, I started to worry.

"Have you ever been to this club?" I asked.

"Mmm-hmm," she said, airily waving her handkerchief. "When your daddy was alive."

"Oh," I said, instantly relieved. Daddy had high standards. "Then it's a decent place?"

"Yes." Then she started humming "Hush, Hush, Sweet Charlotte."

"Stop singing that, Mama."

"I'm not singing, I'm humming."

"You're not telling me everything." I narrowed my eyes. "What sort of place is this?"

"You'll find out," she said. Then she laughed, covering her mouth with the hankie.

Now I was really concerned. I had just asked my mama an open-ended question, and she'd refused the challenge. Our family motto is: Never ask a Little-Hughes woman to elaborate about anything. These Mississippi-Louisiana ladies talk real fast, in high-pitched, nasal voices that are prone to allergies. They invented the run-on sentence. If their conversations were journeys, you'd find yourself on the scenic route—an unpaved road without guardrails.

The antiques club stood on the corner of Daphne and Bellrose. We got out of the car and walked inside. I saw exactly what Mama meant; the club was part museum, part bar. And it was crowded. People sat on stools, laughing and sipping beer—whether they were locals or tourists, I couldn't tell. Hanging on the walls were oxen yolks, cowbells, and rusted farm tools. A rickshaw stood in the corner. Near the bar, I noticed a sign: FRESH BEER TOMORROW. The bartender strolled over and announced that the club was the Bloody Mary capital of the Eastern Shore. "Then bring me one, sugar," Mama said, winking.

I ordered diet Coke, then twirled on the stool, eyeing the cowbells and Jim Beam decanters.

"Didn't I tell you this wasn't regular?" She pointed to the liquor bottles. "Your brother would give his eyeteeth for that decanter."

The bartender appeared and Mama's drink was set before her with a flourish. It was an unusual shade of red, the color that heartbreak ought to be, adorned with a pickled string bean. The glass was so cold it had frosted, and when Mama picked it up, her fingers slid, leaving clear streaks.

"Delicious," she said, plucking out the bean with two fingers and taking a dainty bite. "But not as good as your brother's."

Jimmy's Pickled Green Beans
Yield: 4 pint or 2 quart jars

4 pint (or 2 quart) mason jars;
  new lids and rings
2½ cups white vinegar
2½ cups water
¼ cup kosher salt
4 dried hot peppers (or 2
  tablespoons dried red
  pepper flakes)
8 cloves garlic, peeled

1 tablespoon Tabasco
4 tablespoons dill seeds
2 teaspoons mustard seeds
2 pounds fresh green beans,
  the ends snapped off
1 tablespoon Zatarain's crab
  boil
½ cup sugar, optional

Sterilize the jars. Hold them in the canner. Meanwhile, find a large, nonreactive saucepan. Add the vinegar, water, and salt. Boil. Using tongs, remove one sterilized jar from the canner. Drop in a hot pepper, garlic cloves (2 for each pint jar, 4 for each quart jar), 1 teaspoon dill seeds, and ½ teaspoon mustard seeds. Now start packing in the beans, arranging them straight up and down in the jar. Ladle the hot vinegar solution over beans. Leave a ¼-inch space between the top of the liquid and the rim of the jar. Remove another jar, following the same procedure. Keep filling the jars until you run out of beans. (You can always make more vinegar solution.)

Put on the lids and bands; screw on the bands. Set the jars in a hot-water bath and boil for 10 minutes. Using tongs again, remove jars from the water. Leave on the counter for a couple of hours. Check the lids to make sure they have been sucked down. Tighten the rings, if necessary. You can test the lids by pushing down on them with your fingertip—there should be no wobble or "give," and it should appear indented. Store the jars on a dark, cool shelf. Opened jars will keep in the refrigerator for several weeks. Serve with Bloody Marys.

After a second round of drinks, Mama and I went to the ladies' room, which was dominated by a huge statue of a man—buck naked except for a little fig leaf, poised over its manly part. Mama leaned forward and said, "Look, it's hinged!"

I stepped closer just as Mama lifted the lid. An ear-splitting alarm sounded. It was so loud, tourists in Mobile probably heard it. Mama jumped back, and the leaf snapped shut. From the bar came a spattering of laughter, followed by hoots and applause; I knew we'd been caught. I cracked open the door, staring into the eyes of about fifty crazy Alabama men. With a little gasp, I slammed the door and leaned against it.

"They heard you!" I cried, collapsing against the door.

"Me? For all they know, you're the culprit." She hunkered down, staring intently at the hinge.

"Get away from that statue, Mama," I warned.

"Oh, quit being a wussy," she said. Then she lifted the fig leaf again.

Old Wives' Tales

*Tuck rosemary sprigs under pillows to prevent nightmares. Spilled
salt should always be thrown over the left shoulder. To keep a man
faithful, feed him minced garlic. And whenever women get mad at
each other, they should peel onions.*

—Folk remedy, found in Estelle Brabham's diary, 1902

My great-aunts were born nearly a century ago in the piney
woods of Mississippi, and they grew up without electricity,
plumbing, or penicillin. The nearest hospital was in McComb,
forcing these women to practice folk medicine. They believed in
the merits of apple cider vinegar, claiming a teaspoon a day kept
them young. A distant relative knew a method of "stopping
blood"—it involved reciting a verse from Ezekiel, but she
wouldn't say which one. Hiccups were often cured by putting
sugar on the tongue; if that failed, the hiccuper was forced to
stare at a large butcher knife.

Many cures came from the garden. Luckily, the Brabham
women had green thumbs. Their azaleas grew as tall as houses,
and magnolias scraped against the sky. Sunflowers grew down to
the river's edge, and at night, when the wind blew, the stalks
resembled dancing women. The aunts gardened according to the

moon: Plants that matured on top of the earth were sown when the moon was full; plants maturing underground were sown when the moon showed her dark side. The aunts grew tomatoes and squash; pole beans, bush beans, butter beans; peppers and cucumbers. Summers were spent weeding, harvesting, and canning. It wasn't a hobby; it was survival.

Like the aunts, my mother's thumb is green. During the coldest part of winter, she can step into her garden and find parsley. When she visits, she brings sage for fidelity, rosemary for memory, and lemon thyme for grilled salmon. Aunt Dell is the only Brabham descendant who can't garden. She buys her produce at the grocery, and year-round, she makes vast quantities of lettuce soup. She claims it is a powerful aphrodisiac. "Lettuce was sacred to the phallic god, Min," she told me. To demonstrate, she would squeeze a lettuce core, telling me to pay attention as a thin, milky sap ran between her fingers. "This is mythology and biology," she'd say. "Not superstition. I hate that crap. "

While folk cures were embraced in our family, love medicine was mocked. Still, the aunts knew more than they let on. They would sit on the porch and offer home remedies and advice. I always tried to read between the lines. Never plant peas until you hear the whippoorwill, they'd say. When the moon rises in fog, it means trouble for lovers. If a young girl dreams of wild geese, she will marry many times; but if she dreams of flying swans, she will find her one true beloved. If your romantic dreams are bland, or if you can't remember them in the morning, the aunts would laughingly suggest a passion powder:

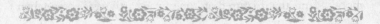

Love Stimulant

1 teaspoon lavender flowers
1 vanilla bean
3 cloves
1 tablespoon chocolate-
  covered coffee beans

Pinch of ground ginger
Pinch of ground cinnamon

Using a mortar and pestle, pulverize the ingredients. Add small pinches to the food of your beloved. If this doesn't work, you might wish to try my Cajun grandmother's method of divining your future husband. On All Souls' Night, carry a candle into the garden. Kneel, and with your eyes closed, find a cabbage. The shape of your chosen vegetable will predict the nature of your future love. Broad leaves symbolize generosity; tightly furled leaves represent stinginess. Bite into the heart of the cabbage. The taste—bitter or sweet—will predict your lover's personality.

Aunt Tempe said that all the secrets and mysteries of love could be found in the center of a cornfield at midnight; but it took a brave soul, not to mention good circulation, to stand in one place for that long. Aunt Dell said it was hogwash. Tempe said she liked to think it was true, even if it did sound crazy. I have always longed to go outside and dance barefoot in the grass, preferably when Venus was rising, and see what would happen.

Tempe seemed to know a lot of love lore. She warned against a bride baking her own wedding cake. It brought bad luck. Many wedding cakes include everyday love stimulants—chocolate, vanilla, and ginger. No matter what sort of cake the bride chooses (a spice cake can cause a spicy relationship), she should preserve a slice, keeping it in a safe place. This will ensure the love of her husband.

On the other hand, if you wish to get rid of an unwanted suitor, douse yourself in camphor. You can also carry a raw turnip in your purse—or better yet, feed stewed turnips to the crazed lover. Always serve eggplant to a man before you leave him. Just make certain you're ready to depart, because impulsive acts have consequences. They can lead to regret; in severe cases, they might damage the heart. The aunts had a cure for that, too.

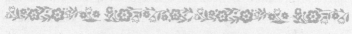

Remedy for a Lonely Heart

3 pounds orange
   marmalade—any brand
One 8-ounce jar maraschino
   cherries, drained
1 cup golden raisins

½ cup currants
1 cup walnuts, coarsely
   chopped
3½ tablespoons fresh lemon
   juice

Mix all ingredients. Spoon into sterilized jelly jars. Tie with a bow and give to a friend.

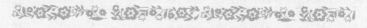

૪ ૪

Infidelity was a hot topic in our family. In 1934, my sainted grandfather showed a wee bit too much interest in a waitress at Bud and Lila's Cafe. When my Mimi found out, she put a pearl-handled pistol in her pocketbook and drove down to the restaurant. Two days later, the waitress left town, driving off in a battered Chevy truck.

The aunts blamed this flirtation on watermelon. They claimed any man could be seduced by its juice. My cousin Lula, who has a penchant for marrying faithless men, swears by lemons. She calls it a love fruit. Lemon pie is effective, she says, but a lemonade infusion is even better. Add sugar for optimum results.

Over the years, I heard many home remedies for a wandering husband. A sprig of rosemary in a man's shoe might induce fidelity. Then again, it might only cure his smelly feet. A rose quartz, worn close to the heart, is said to strengthen a weak marriage. Aunt Dell suggests saltpeter. My brother claims that a machete works wonders. When placed on the wife's bedside table, it often has a profound effect upon the male psyche.

Better Than Sex Cake
Yield: 12 servings

1 box Duncan Hines butter cake mix

One 8-ounce package chocolate chips

One 8-ounce package pecans, chopped

1 box instant vanilla pudding mix

½ box unsweetened German chocolate, grated

One 8-ounce carton sour cream

½ cup Wesson oil

½ cup milk

4 eggs

1 stick unsalted butter, room temperature

Preheat the oven to 350 degrees. Mix all the ingredients with the cake mix. Pour into a greased and floured Bundt pan. Bake 1 hour. When the cake is cool, make the icing.

To Make the Icing

One 8-ounce package cream
   cheese, at room temperature
1 box confectioners' sugar

1 teaspoon vanilla
Chopped nuts
Flaked coconut

Cream together the cream cheese and sugar. Add the vanilla. Ice the
cake. Sprinkle with the nuts and coconut.

    This cake is so good you may feel compelled to mash your face
in it—I know two people who have. Later, they said they didn't
know what came over them. One minute they were staring at the
cake and the next they had icing up their noses. One July Fourth,
I brought this dessert to a family picnic. The relatives gathered
around, nibbling crumbs.

    "Get a grip," Aunt Dell said, snorting. "'Better Than Sex Cake'
isn't."

    "Isn't what?" said Lula.

    "Better than sex!" cried Dell. She waved her hands, knocking
over a salt shaker. "This cake can't hold a candle to the real thing."

    "Not to be rude, Dell, but how would *you* know?" Lula reached
for the cake, cutting a huge slice.

    "I know things that would curl your hair," said Dell, nodding.
"Speaking of which, this cake is better than a home permanent.
But that's about all." She winked at me. Then she took a pinch of
salt and threw it over her left shoulder.

    "I thought you weren't superstitious," I said.

    "I'm not," said Dell, indignant. "But it never hurts to be prepared."

Honey

> *The honeybee,* Apis mellifera, *visits fifty to a hundred blossoms each day before returning to the hive. If they get confused and return to the wrong hive, they risk death.*
>
> —Old beekeeper, telling bee lore to novices, Middle Tennessee, 1982

From the driveway, I watched two astronauts climb out of a Chevy truck. They wore sneakers, gloves, and white canvas suits. Their wide-brimmed hats were covered with a yellow mesh veil, which zipped around their throats. In the back of the truck sat a white chest with four drawers. "Did you buy some furniture?" I asked my husband. This was rural Tennessee, a place where anything was possible—you might dash down to the local antiques mall and spot country music stars Pam Tillis or Garth Brooks; or you might get a midnight call from one of your neighbors asking if you'd seen alien spaceships hovering over her pond.

"No, I bought a beehive," said Will, rubbing his hands together. After twenty years of marriage, I knew what he was thinking: jars of clear, wildflower honey, all lined up in a sunny window. Each jar would have a label: Will's Honey Pot.

As I stared at the ominous white boxes, my heart sped up. The suited men were scooting the hive to the edge of the truck bed. A few angry bees hummed in the air, but the men seemed oblivious. On the count of three, the men lifted the box high, grunting with the effort. They backed it out of the truck, and then trudged down the driveway. Trailed by a dozen bees, the hive bobbed up and down. Following at a discreet distance, I watched the men carry the box down the length of the yard. With a flourish, they set it down at the property line—overlooking a pond and a shady cedar forest.

"I bought us each a bee suit," Will said, walking up to me.

"I don't want one." I shook my head. "I hate bees."

"You don't know the first thing about them," he said.

"I don't want to."

"That's silly." He thoughtfully watched the men as they trudged back up the hill, circled by bees. "I can't wait to extract the honey," Will said. The next time you get a cough, I'll fix you a syrup. Don't look at me like that. People have been beekeeping for thousands of years, since the Stone Age."

"Why don't we just buy honey at the store?" I asked. My mama would say that when a man seeks out the sweeter things in life, he might attract more than bees; but I had different worries.

"You have no sense of adventure," he said. "But I do."

That whole summer my adventures were mainly culinary. The bee men left us a jar of strained wildflower honey. I began experimenting with marinades for seafood and chicken, and by the end of August, I had hit upon a sublime recipe.

Honey Teriyaki Marinade
Yield: Approximately 3 cups

1 cup honey	1½ teaspoons fresh gingerroot,
1 cup soy sauce	peeled and grated
1 cup sake	1 teaspoon sesame oil
1 large clove garlic, minced	

Mix all of the ingredients. Pour over salmon, shrimp, or chicken. Marinate three hours or overnight. Grill as usual.

✂ ✄

I left the bees to the devil, but Will would occasionally put on his suit and walk to the edge of the woods. He'd circle the white box until he was satisfied that his colony was flourishing. Then he'd traipse back to the house. He had grandiose plans: We could enter our jars in the county fair; why, we could even peddle them at local groceries! Soon Will's Honey Pot would be distributed nationwide. Then he could retire from medicine and take up bee-keeping full-time.

It wasn't long before the bees outgrew their box. There are roughly 40,000 bees per hive, which meant one thing to me: A single hive possessed an indeterminate number of stings. I wasn't thrilled. When I explained this to Will, he said, "Get some courage, woman. Go put on your bee suit."

That September he announced he was adding another drawer to the hive. It was late in the afternoon, and the sun was just starting to drop into the cedars. The sky glowed orange, and the air itself seemed too warm, as if it might ignite. I could almost taste the colors: tangerine, butterscotch, sour cherry. Wild honey.

In the garage, Will suited up, stabbing his arms into the uniform. He put on his helmet, dragging the zipper across his throat. "Are you coming with me?" he asked.

I shook my head.

He sighed, then slogged toward the woods. In the white uniform, he looked extremely odd, less like a husband and more like an alien. I stood by the forsythia hedge, keeping a wary distance, and watched him build a fire in his little smoker, using leaves and twigs. He waved it back and forth around the hive's opening. Then, with a curved tool, he pried off the top layer of the box and set it on the grass.

"Don't be so scared," he called. "Get your suit on and come help me. Bees don't fly after dusk."

"I'm not scared," I yelled. I just didn't want to be stung. Besides, it was still daylight. Earlier in the summer, I'd walked barefoot to the clothesline, and I'd stepped on a bee. The pain was so shocking that I tossed a basket of damp sheets into the air and ran screaming back to the house. I wasn't about to get near those bees. Now, watching my fearless husband, I remembered reading that smoke had a calming effect on the creatures, and sure enough, the bees seemed indifferent to the dismantling. They crawled on the grass, all around Will's shoes. He was wearing black socks, but I could see the bees moving past his ankles. Pretty soon the lower half of his body was dark brown. Will cursed and stamped his feet. I seemed to recall something in the literature about the proper colors to wear around bees; but there were so many cautions I couldn't remember them all.

The bees were drawn to Will's socks. A mini-swarm was beginning around his ankles. He started dancing the Watusi, then he let out a scream; it ripped through the air, lifting the hair on my arms. In olden days, the French thought bee stings were powerful aphrodisiacs. Now, watching Will, I knew the French were mistaken. Will took off running, flinging the smoker, his hands slapping his helmet.

He raced past me. Over his screams, I could hear the bees going *zzzt, zzzt, zzzt!* He ran in a circle, then crashed into the forsythia hedge. He fell to his knees. The bees circled above him, humming a war dance. Clawing his way up the bush, he struggled to his feet and charged toward our neighbor's pond. Unfortunately, this neighbor also believed in UFOs. She thought the U.S. government kept an alien on ice somewhere in New Mexico. And she was always seeing flashing lights over my house—a sign that abduction was imminent.

Will emitted out another scream. "Black socks!" he wailed, followed by a string of expletives. I remembered what the bee books had advised: Always wear white in their presence; dark colors make them violent. As Will streaked through our neighbor's honeysuckle, he let out a pathetic scream. The vines had snagged his yellow veil. With a violent heave, he ripped free. I followed at a discreet distance, watching him stumble toward the pond. His arms and legs flailing, he leaped into the water. It took him with a dazzling slap. In the dusky light, I anxiously watched as he splashed and moaned, trying to drown the bees. Our neighbor stepped out of her house, one hand over her heart. Her dyed red hair poked out of a purple turban. "What on *earth*," she said.

"It's just Will," I called.

"Well, thank goodness," she said, watching him thrash in the water. "What happened to the poor boy?"

"Mutiny," I said. "His bees turned on him."

"How perfectly ghastly. But bees will do that," she said. "I saw him running, and it put me in mind of *The Andromeda Strain*. You ever see that movie?"

I nodded.

"Scared me to *death*," she said, gesturing at Will. "I might have to take a pill."

I walked to the edge of the pond. Will's helmet was rakishly askew. I started to say something about aphrodisiacs, courage, and a sense of adventure, but he was slogging out of the muddy water. A lone bee circled his head.

"Miss Lee?" he cried, lifting his arms from the water. "Where are you?"

"Right here, honey," I said, and held out my hand.

The Cabbage-Eating Ghost

All Southerners are the great-grandchildren of ghosts.
—William Faulkner

Aunt Lilly was a war bride, acquired by Uncle Toby when he was stationed in Fort Benning, Georgia. Lilly is an aristocratic woman who runs around with the blue bloods of Tangipahoa Parish. She belongs to two bridge clubs and has a standing appointment at Casa Bonita Salon. She belongs to the ladies' league, volunteers at the hospital, and plays the organ at First Presbyterian. She and Toby live in a neoclassical house on Iris Street, and it is filled with antiques—mostly Empire with a touch of the Louis, but somehow Lilly pulled it together. China is her special passion. Although she adores Wedgwood and Spode, she has a weakness for majolica and Flow Blue—all frightfully expensive.

Early in the summer, while browsing in a dusty shop in Covington, Lilly found a Flow Blue chamber pot. It didn't have a chip and when she turned it over, the mark revealed it to be genuine Flow Blue. It was marked $25, the steal of the century. A piece like that would normally sell for $250. "I'll take it," she told the elderly clerk. "Does it have a pedigree?"

"It's old," said the clerk. "That's all I know."

A ruffled apricot umbrella also caught Lilly's attention. It was very handsome, with a tortoiseshell handle. This time the clerk spoke up. "That umbrella dates back to 1879," she said. "It's in mint condition."

"Then why is it only ten dollars?" asked Lilly.

"Don't ask me." The clerk shrugged. "I don't price things. I just work here."

Lilly whipped out her checkbook. Then she drove home and found Toby in the backyard, mowing the lawn. She pulled on a pair of heavy garden gloves and knelt down beside the potting shed, yanking weeds by the roots. By the time she remembered the antiques, it was dark. As she and Toby carried in the sacks, Lilly vaguely remembered an old saying—carry in an antique after dark and you'll surely carry in a ghost; but she didn't believe that nonsense.

In the master bedroom, Lilly set the chamber pot on the mantel. She propped the umbrella against a carved Victorian chair. Tomorrow, Lilly thought, she'd put it on the hall tree, where she displayed her vintage hats. A lot of people—Toby included—thought the house seemed staged and not real homey. And it did resemble a museum. Every Christmas, Lilly's house was on the annual tour of homes, and she would dress up in lacy old clothes and personally greet each guest.

Now she patted the umbrella. "I got it for a steal," she told Toby.

"That's nice, honey," he said.

That night Lilly fried cabbage for supper. As she cooked, she thought she heard a thump from the bedroom. "That you, Toby?" she called.

No answer. She walked up to the bedroom. The umbrella wasn't next to the mantel. It was on the other side of the room; but the chamber pot had inched its way toward the bay window. "That's odd," she said. She put the umbrella back against the mantel, then shoved the pot back against the wall. From downstairs, Toby called, "Honey? I think supper's about to burn."

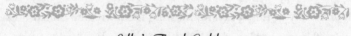

Lilly's Fried Cabbage
Yield: 3 or 4 servings

In a heavy skillet, fry 4 strips of bacon. Remove when crisp and set aside. Core the cabbage and divide into quarters. Place in the skillet, cooking over a medium flame. Add a pinch of sugar. Salt and pepper to taste. Gently stir, allowing the cabbage to wilt and brown. Garnish with the crumbled bacon.

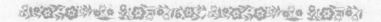

After supper, Lilly was so exhausted she left the pot of cabbage on the stove, thinking she'd wash it the next morning. She and Toby climbed into bed. While Toby snored and Lilly tossed, the smell of fried cabbage drifted through the house. It hovered in the corners, finding its way to the attic, where it wafted along the timbers.

Four hours later, Lilly was awakened by a burst of light. She sat up in bed and blinked. An old man rose out of the fireplace. Then he pushed a plow across the room, vanishing into a highboy. Lilly wasn't frightened, but she sensed a deep fatigue, and a long-forgotten sorrow. She turned to Toby and said, "I think I saw a ghost."

"Hush up!" Toby growled, yanking the covers over his head.

"It's gone now," Lilly said, squinting at the highboy. She settled against the pillow and fell into a deep sleep, and if she dreamed at all, she had lost all memory of it by morning. But she had a clear recollection of the farmer pushing the plow. Over breakfast, pouring coffee for Toby, she described the ghost in detail.

"Why did you tell me to hush?" she asked. "You acted so odd."

"Because I saw the ghost, too," he said. "And it spooked me. It was just as you said. But it seemed to me that he had a face like Abraham Lincoln."

"Yes, he did." Lilly nodded. "He had a beard, and his cheekbones were all sunk in."

"A real tall fellow," said Toby.

"Over six feet," said Lilly.

"Do you think we can move that chamber pot to another room?" he asked, stirring his coffee.

"Why, of course." She took a bite of toast. "But what if the ghost came in with the umbrella?"

"I think it was hungry," said Toby, staring at the empty cabbage pot. "It ate all the leftovers."

"Ghosts don't eat," Lilly scoffed. She had a cousin in Atlanta who'd bought an infested grandfather clock. The spirits smashed Waterford goblets and crept up and down the staircase at three A.M. And she knew a cousin who bought a Victorian bed in Chattanooga. It gave the cousin violent nightmares, forcing him to sleep on the floor. He ended up taking the bed to Goodwill.

But Lilly had never heard of a ghost who stayed for supper. She wondered if the strong odor of cabbage might have been responsible, arousing powerful longings. If there *were* ghosts. Now she looked at Toby and said, "Maybe we have rats."

On ten separate occasions, Lilly fried cabbage, pointedly leaving the leftovers on the stove. Each time, she and Toby were awakened by the light, and the sallow-faced ghost marched across the bedroom, pushing his plow and fading into the highboy. In the morning, the cabbage was gone.

"Wonder if the ghost came with the umbrella or the chamber pot?" asked Toby.

"I'd bet the pot," said Lilly. "But whoever is in that umbrella might like cabbage, too."

❧ ❧

Toward the end of summer, when I was visiting relatives in Tangipahoa Parish, Lilly invited me for lunch. As I stepped past the potting shed, I noticed it was half hidden by wisteria. Weeds had sprung up around the climbing roses, choking out the blooms. The shed was barely two years old. Lilly had been decorating it in the style of Martha Stewart: mossy clay pots, cast-iron urns, egg baskets. A collage of antique flower prints lined the walls. Rumor had it that *Southern Living* was driving up to photograph the shed, but she said they'd laugh if they saw it now.

"What happened?" I asked.

"Oh, it's a long story," she said, pulling me down the path. "I've got a ghost trapped in there. A cabbage-eating ghost."

"You're teasing, right?" I tried to smile. Then I looked back at the shed.

"No, it's true. Once a week, I feed it," she said. "Lately it's had a taste for coleslaw. In fact, that's what we're having for lunch. It's the hungriest ghost I've ever heard of." She leaned toward me. "Do you want it? The ghost, not the slaw. He comes with an umbrella and a nice chamber pot. They're genuine antiques, of course."

"I don't need any extra trouble," I said. I turned around and stared at the potting shed.

"Ghosts aren't so bad," she said cheerfully.

I just stared. She looped her arm in mind and together we walked toward the house. "But if you ever change your mind," she told me, glancing back at the shed, "you know where to come."

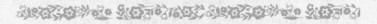

The Margaret Mitchell Bed

If Scarlett O'Hara had made gingersnap cookies for Ashley, she could have stolen him from Melanie. And if she'd fed them to Sherman, he would never have burned Atlanta.

—Mrs. Hawkes, antiques dealer and *Gone with the Wind* buff

Mrs. Hawkes is known around town as the antique lady. This is not because of her age, although she is quite elderly, but because many years ago, Mrs. Hawkes sold antiques from her home. On Sundays, she would drive home from church, and people would be waiting in her driveway, hoping to buy a cherry sideboard or a gateleg table. While customers browsed in bedrooms, opening closets and drawers, Mrs. Hawkes stationed herself in the kitchen, mashing potatoes for Sunday dinner.

A few years ago, after a series of family tragedies, Mrs. Hawkes decided to sell many of her antiques. They were rumored to be the finest in middle Tennessee, including a bed that had once belonged to Margaret Mitchell. Will and I were invited to a private viewing on Sunday afternoon, the day before the public auction. The sale wasn't very private, as everyone in town showed up, and we had to wait in a line that led from the front porch to the mailbox. Finally, we stepped into the crowded parlor. I worried that we would never find the famous bed, and Will worried that someone would buy it before we could. Ladies from the Mary Martha Missionary Circle were stationed around the house, making sure none of the Dresden or Staffordshire plates disappeared; but the crowd was docile, lulled by the scent of orange oil and Old English scratch cover.

Mrs. Hawkes broke loose from a group of women; then she led me and Will down a long, low-ceilinged hall. As we passed the dining room, she gestured at a cherry corner cupboard, whispering that it was a steal at $5,000. A mahogany sideboard was being sacrificed for a mere $3,500.

My heart sank. I hadn't expected such steep prices. Mrs. Hawkes glanced over her shoulder, crooking her finger at Will. "Come on now; I've got something to show you."

She led us to a bedroom with floral walls and a plush green carpet. "This," she said proudly, spreading her arms, "is the Margaret Mitchell bed."

Will and I blinked. It was a massive double bed, forbiddingly high, requiring steps to reach it. "It's solid cherry," said Mrs. Hawkes, running her fingers along a thick post. "I bought it nearly fifty years ago from a man who got it from the childhood home of Miss Mitchell."

"So it wasn't her actual bed," said Will.

"No, just a bed in her childhood home," said Mrs. Hawkes. "But if I can authenticate it, I can get upward of a hundred thousand dollars."

"That much?" said Will. "What if it's a fake?"

"Do you think it's real?" I asked.

"Well, that's what I was told." Mrs. Hawkes smiled, lifting her shoulders. "And I believe it with all my heart. But you never know."

"Where is the man you bought it from?" asked Will.

"Oh, he's been dead for several decades." Mrs. Hawkes leaned toward the bed. "Notice the patina, how fine it is. I almost lost this bed, you know. It nearly burned up in a fire. Notice how dark the footboard is? I had it refinished, but still—" She broke off.

"It means a lot to you," I said.

"Lord, yes. This bed has a lot of history. My poor little husband spent his last days right here." She reached up and patted the mattress. Then she cut her eyes at me. "But he didn't die in it. Just look at these unusual posts. They go all the way to the ceiling."

"It's handsome," I said. The wood was shiny, smelling faintly of lemons. "But it's way out of our price range."

"Well, that's all right," she said. "But if you change your mind, you know where to find me. Just don't wait too long."

On the way home, Will said, "I want that bed."

"We can't afford it," I protested. Will was a reckless buyer. Once, at an antiques mall in Carthage, Tennessee, he had lusted after a battered French dresser that had belonged to Tipper Gore; he would have bought it, too, but it wouldn't fit in his car.

"Maybe Mrs. Hawkes will come down on the price," he said.

"She's got a long way to go," I pointed out.

"You need that bed," he told me. "You're a writer. Margaret Mitchell was a writer."

"But I'm obscure," I said.

"Yes, but you might write something good," he said. "Eventually."

Then he reminded me of that time he'd saved my life. In New Orleans, I'd stepped into Royal Street, and was heading straight into the path of a speeding taxi when Will yanked me back. He pulled so hard, I fell down. I got up, brushing off my jeans, and he said, "You owe me, Miss Lee. I saved your life."

Now he pounded his fist against his palm. "I want that bed," he cried.

൞ ൡ

Three years later, Mrs. Hawkes telephoned. She had endured another tragedy and she was downscaling again. "I'm sacrificing the Margaret Mitchell bed," she said. "And I'm giving you first shot at it."

Naturally we drove right over. She led us to the bedroom. Will walked around, taking measurements. Truth be told, we didn't need another bed, especially one this enormous, and it would look cumbersome in our small bedroom; but my husband had a wild glint in his eyes.

"I'll sell it cheap," she said.

"How cheap?" Will blinked.

"Let's talk about it over coffee," Mrs. Hawkes said, smiling. In her sunny kitchen, she served gingersnap cookies. They were crisp at the edges, moist in the center, with a poignant bite of ginger. Will popped two in his mouth, then closed his eyes, chewing and making guttural sounds.

"Men just love these cookies," said Mrs. Hawkes. "The recipe came from a Georgia woman who claimed to know Margaret Mitchell. She used to make a batch of cookies and take them to the author while she was working on her book."

"It was a long novel. She must have eaten a lot of gingersnaps," said Will, filling his pockets with cookies.

"I'm sure she did, honey," said Mrs. Hawkes.

Thinking I'd never get my hands on the bed, I brazenly asked for the recipe. Mrs. Hawkes presented it to me on an index card studded with a magnolia decal.

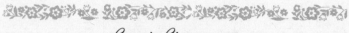

Georgia Gingersnaps
Yield: 5 dozen

1½ sticks unsalted butter, melted and cooled	2 cups flour
1 cup sugar plus more for rolling	1 teaspoon baking soda
	½ teaspoon ground cloves
¼ cup unsulphured molasses	¾ teaspoon ground ginger
1 egg	¾ teaspoon ground cinnamon
	½ teaspoon salt

Mix the cooled butter with the 1 cup sugar, molasses, and egg. Mix well. Sift together the remaining ingredients. Stir into the sugar mixture. Cover the dough and chill several hours. Roll into 1-inch balls. Then roll each ball in more granulated sugar. Bake at 375 degrees for 8 to 10 minutes. Remove from pans immediately and cool on wire racks.

Twenty minutes later, the bed was ours. As we walked out to the truck, Mrs. Hawkes called me back. She put a large dog fig-

Gumbo Ya-Ya

urine in my hands. "This is for you," she said. "It came out of the childhood home of Jacqueline Kennedy."

"Really?" I cradled the figurine.

"That's what I was told," said Mrs. Hawkes. "But you never know."

Inheritance

No one ever asks for my recipes. But I'll give you one anyway. To remember me by. Take ½ cup red wine vinegar, ½ cup brown sugar, 3 tablespoons ketchup, 3 tablespoons Worcestershire, 1 tablespoon prepared mustard, and 1 clove garlic, minced. Whisk. Pour over steaks and marinate for 3 to 4 hours or overnight. The longer you marinate, the better.

> —Aunt Dell, discussing food at a funeral, Dijon, Louisiana, 1982

At family gatherings, Aunt Dell likes to read tabloid newspapers. She'll sit on a bar stool, one leg swinging wildly, and she'll say, "Listen up. 'Elvis is alive, being held against his will in a Memphis basement.'"

"He's dead," says my husband. "I have a colleague who helped perform the autopsy."

"You did? I mean, he *did*?" Dell's mouth opens, revealing a row of silver fillings.

"Give it a rest, Dell," says Mama.

"Well, listen to this," Dell says, rattling the paper. "'Lust causes heart attacks.'"

"So does butter," says Mama.

"'Dog dressed like baby kills its owners,'" she says. "'Thong bikini saves shark-attack victim!' 'Church supper sickens three hundred, kills one.' "

While most of the aunts were widows, Dell was a confirmed bachelorette. Then a life-changing event occurred. Shortly after her fiftieth birthday, during the coldest winter on record, the pipes froze and burst in her pink-and-green house. Next, the ceiling collapsed. The insurance company sent out an adjuster named Billy Nolan. He didn't seem to mind Dell's jumbled house, and when she invited him to stay for supper, he eagerly accepted. He seemed genuinely amused by the hairless cats. Over meat loaf and mashed potatoes, he told Dell that he restored old cars. He lived on a sixty-acre farm with his mama, in a house with ceilings and plumbing.

After the wedding, Dell moved in with Billy and his mama, who asked to be called Mrs. Nolan. The move required two weeks of intense labor, calling for untold trips to the local dump. One afternoon Dell showed up with her hairless cats, and the Nolans' chickens flew up into the trees. "That's all right," Billy said, and Dell kissed him on the lips. But it wasn't all right. After the hens began laying eggs in the iris beds, Mrs. Nolan took her son aside. She hated cats, and Dell's animals were particularly hideous. They were bound to claw the furniture, and they tormented the chickens. All of her best layers had flown into the woods. Couldn't Billy, her own baby son, do something?

Billy said he'd try. On weekends, the newlyweds went to Dell's old pink-and-green house and loaded the truck with Grecian statues and boxes. Then they would drive back to the Nolan farm, lugging Dell's things into the house. During the week, Dell unpacked, and the living room began to resemble an antiques mall. Fiesta dishes were stacked on the floor next to fringed lamp shades and McCoy vases. "This junk makes me dizzy," said Mrs. Nolan. "Can't you do something, Billy?"

"One thing at a time, Mama," he said. "One thing at a time."

When a stray tom wandered onto the farm, all of the female cats simultaneously went into heat, yowling all night long. It became clear that Billy had no intention of talking to his wife. The old woman gathered up her nerve and confronted Dell.

"Billy has cars and chickens." Dell shrugged. "I have cats and antiques. Everyone has to have something."

The old woman looked around the yard. It was littered with cars, all in various states of disrepair. A 1952 Cadillac had rusted out, and weeds were growing through the steering wheel. "Cars don't run up veterinarian bills," she told Dell. "Cars don't pee in the corners."

"I have quilts that are worth a fortune," said Dell, her eyes flashing.

"I'd pay a fortune to have them hauled off!"

When the women started arguing, Billy crawled under one of the cars, whistling and tinkering. Later, he started the engine of a van, and a cat screamed. He shut off the motor, but it was too late. Billy put the remains in a sack and buried it by the river. The next morning, when Dell called the cats to breakfast, she kept counting heads, puzzled about the mysterious disappearance of her favorite kitten, Eustace. When she asked Billy if he knew anything about it, he patted his wife's hand and said, "Honey, you know that cats lead violent lives."

The mother-in-law burned vanilla candles to hide the over-powering aroma that emanated from the litter boxes. She took to her bedroom, plugging gaps in the door with tea towels, and refused to come out. "Those litter boxes," she'd say, fanning her face with a magazine. "It just takes my breath."

When a flea nipped the mother-in-law's leg, she moved to a garden apartment in Dijon, leaving her son and Dell in what she called "that hellhole." Thereafter, my favorite aunt entered a long, catless period—she shipped every last animal to a breeder in Tucson, Arizona. And she talked about opening an antiques store.

Without the mother-in-law and the cats, Dell's marriage to the old mechanic seemed blissful. You could see them catching a Sunday afternoon matinee, sharing a bag of popcorn, or sitting in the same booth at Bud and Lila's Cafe, feeding each other French fries.

Then one Sunday Dell came home from church and found Billy Nolan's legs protruding from a red Impala. The chickens were running wild, and the rooster was strutting on the roof. "Billy?" said Dell, staring at her husband's legs. No answer, no movement. She stepped forward. "Billy Nolan?" she cried. "You better stop fooling me!"

※ ※

"The jack collapsed," Dell said at the funeral home, dabbing her eyes. "It crushed him." She was sitting in the first row, dressed in a black tablecloth. Lula and the aunts hovered protectively. On the other side of the room, the mother-in-law was shouting. "My

Billy was a genius with carburetors," she cried. "He always set up two jacks before he'd crawl beneath a car."

"Just ignore her," said Lula, patting Dell's shoulder.

The mother-in-law got up from her chair and charged, but two bull-necked women restrained her. "Let me go," old Mrs. Nolan said, wrenching herself free. She ran down the aisle and threw herself against the coffin. It caused such a stir that the undertaker was forced to prematurely shut the lid.

Because the death was accidental, Dell collected double indemnity from the insurance policy. The mama tried to sue, on the basis that her son hadn't been lucid when he'd married the hussy; but a judge ruled in Dell's favor. Not too long afterward, Dell drove up to Lula's house with a silver Airstream tacked onto her brand-new Lincoln Continental. She'd come to say good-bye. "I'm selling both houses and moving to Florida," she said. "I may be gone a long while."

She blew a kiss, then hit the gas and drove off, spitting gravel. When the dust cleared, the Airstream was a dot on the road, glinting in the sun. Then Dell was gone. "Double indemnity," said Lula. "How lucky can a girl get?"

"Huh," said Mama. "I'll bet Billy Nolan had a heart attack, and Dell found him dead. I'll bet she dragged him under that car and kicked out that jack, squashing him like a bug."

"Or maybe he wasn't dead when she found him," Lula whispered.

A month later, the Realtors had an open house at the Nolans' old farm. The mother-in-law had spread rumors about Dell's hoard. Everyone was curious. The agents walked through the rooms, stumbling over debris, sidestepping bone china oyster plates. Several ladies gathered in the living room, trying to decide if they should call an auctioneer or a junk man. While they argued, a thousand fleas rose up from the carpet. A few Realtors slapped their ankles. "Mosquitoes?" said one.

"No, fleas!" cried another.

The women stampeded. One lady, a member of the million-dollar club, later counted 108 bite marks on her legs. An exterminator was summoned, but even he was forced to evacuate. He planned to do the fumigation in stages, fighting his way through the house, wielding his power sprayer like a machete. They say he charged through the front door and was never seen again. By this time the fleas were airborne, peppering the air with an audible hum.

On dark, windless nights, they say, you can hear the buzzing, and it almost sounds human. If you strain to listen, you'll swear the fleas are crying their little hearts out. Whether they miss Dell or the cats, it's impossible to say. Mama and I miss her terribly. And when the moon is full and the highway is empty, sometimes we imagine a Lincoln Continental pulling an Airstream and racing down the highway. "Why, it's Dell," we cry.

But it never is.

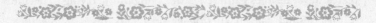

How Southerners Talk

Southerners speak real slow because they come from a land where food is savored. People who eat fast, like nurses and Yankees, run the risk of getting choked. Also, chewing the fat isn't liable to make you plump. Talking is a good way to burn calories.

—Big Mama, owner of Long Tall Sally's Clothes: A Shop for Women of Stature, Dijon, Louisiana, 1998

Somewhere south of the Mason-Dixon line, the air begins to subtly change. This is the milieu of the weird and the wonderful, where Elvis impersonators, all decked out in sequins, shop at the local Piggly Wiggly. It's where the new McDonald's was built right next door to a genuine haunted house. And where old bathtubs are converted into shrines for the Blessed Virgin. It is also a food zone—if people aren't cooking, then they're talking about food. Right this minute, from New Iberia to Memphis, from Charlotte to Savannah, mouthwatering dishes are being served, discussed, and consumed.

I come from a long line of eccentric Southerners who love to eat and talk—frequently at the same time. This has been a trial and tribulation for my mama, who has required the Heimlich maneuver at every family gathering. Once we were playing charades and Mama was fluttering her hands, darting around the room. "A bird?" we said. "No, airplane! A person, place, or thing? One syllable or two, Mama?"

Mama turned a lurid shade of gray and pointed to a cut-glass dish. My father understood at once. He leaped up, applied therapeutic pressure to her abdomen, and out shot a bourbon ball, striking the wall with a reassuring splat. Today, if you asked her about it, she would say I'd made it up, that I'd lived with fiction so long that I couldn't tell the truth if I had to. No, I had to mix it up like some kind of crazy recipe.

Then I'd have to tell you another story, about the time she was beachcombing in Acapulco. She wasn't even swimming; she was fully dressed. As Mama leaned over to pick up a shell, a giant wave curved over her head, scooped her up, and swept her out to sea. Just for the record, she is an excellent swimmer. But she was clutching her canvas pocketbook, which weighed about fifty pounds and contained passports and the family loot. Now her pocketbook was filling with seawater and no amount of kicking or dog-paddling could keep her head above water.

Still, she held on, thinking how she'd never live it down if she lost that purse. How would she explain it at customs? I expect she would have done it in her inimitable style, which is very much like a Hollywood reporter, but with a Mississippi flair. "Well, sir," she'd say, "you see, I was beachcombing? And I had just found the prettiest little pink and blue shells? Only they aren't so little, they're right big. I forget what they're called. It starts with an *a*, and it rhymes with bologna. Aunt Dell had one. Dell, Mimi's baby sister's daughter, who used to stand behind the kitchen door and pray? Dell, who shaved off her eyebrows because it was such a pain to pluck them; Dell, who has gotten so fat she has to iron her pants in the driveway; Dell, who pulled an Airstream to Florida and has never been heard from again. Anyhow, a great big wave swept over my head and carried me out to sea. Well, not a big wave, but a powerful one nonetheless."

In truth, Mama held on to her purse, and just when she stopped struggling and began to sink down in the polluted Pacific, two Mexican lifeguards pulled her from the water, pocketbook and all.

Stories like this abound in our family, sometimes in excruciating detail. These details are like ingredients in gumbo: Leave out one thing and you risk losing some flavor and spice. Like the time my husband went scuba diving and we all thought he'd drowned. A panic ensued. By the time we'd color-coordinated his funeral, he surfaced a few yards down the beach, oblivious to the commotion.

Aunt Dell was a source of juicy tales. One winter her water pipes froze and burst. Rather than call a repairman, Dell just *moved*. The other relatives lived wacky lives. I remember when my cousin Lula decided to buy a new car. She was a little shook up from her divorce, so she barely paid attention when her daughter was rubbing her fingers over the knobs.

"Mom, what's all these bumpy things on the buttons?" she asked. Lula felt the ridges with her fingertips and said, "That's for the Braille drivers, honey."

In every Southern family there's probably enough fodder for a dozen novels. Stories, recipes, and secrets are passed down orally—the history of a clan, complete with triumphs, follies, and even a few unsolved mysteries. Any curious Southerner can uproot buried truths—you just need to know where to dig. I keep meaning to write about the time Mama was having a party, and my brother put goldfish in the toilet. And what about the time Aunt Dell ordered a pizza, and when the man asked what kind she wanted, Dell said, "Oh, just surprise me!"

In my family, funerals are occasions for storytelling—usually at a family member's expense. Usually that person is me. I remember when my grandmother died, and everyone was gathered in Aunt Joyce's kitchen drinking Jax beer and eating jambalaya. Then the family started in on the time I took dancing lessons in New Orleans, and at the recital I burst into tears and Mama had to lead me from the stage. Another time I took a ferry to Ship Island and got smacked by a green wave and lost my bathing suit. "You always did have trouble keeping your swimsuits on," she said. Then she told everybody how she'd recently cleaned out my childhood closet and found a tin of butter cookies, its contents withered and mummified.

"She was bad about hoarding food," Mama said. Then she put her hand under my chin. "You've come a long way. I remember when you couldn't pronounce 'oregano' "

"She called it 'orry-GAN-o,' " said Aunt Lula. "Kinda like what the winged monkeys sang in *The Wizard of Oz*."

"You're no better," said Dell, eyeing Lula. "When you were twenty-four you didn't know how to pronounce 'impotent.' You went around saying, 'That fellow sure is important.' "

"In those days," said Lula, "I didn't *need* to pronounce it."

In our family, a meal at Mama's house is a lesson in genealogy. Each dish has a pedigree, going back many generations. As you follow her voice, you'll find yourself suffering from motion sickness. It's like traveling in the mountains—the driver won't pay attention to the curvy road, and one hand is barely touching the wheel. The other hand is either wildly gesturing or else poking you in the arm. Forget about slipping a word in edgewise. All you can do is wait for the ride to end. As you sweep down byroads and gravel roads, you find yourself traveling backward in time until, finally, you are standing at the gates of the Garden of Eden. Naturally you get a full rundown on what Eve is cooking for supper.

Whether it's genes or environment, I couldn't escape stories—or recipes—if I tried. Mostly I collect them like so many shells. I bring them home, wash them off, and glue them together. Now, when Mama calls me long-distance, and she starts telling me about her day, I roll up my sleeves and pour a deep cup of coffee. She tells me about her cat and her garden and all of the flowers and all of the herbs and all of the meals she has cooked, right down to the teaspoons. Our conversations are long and one-sided, and they are far too spicy for either one of us to get bored.

"Are you listening?" she'll say in a suspicious tone. "Are you still there?"

"I'm listening, Mama," I tell her. "I'm listening."

Recipe Index

Applesauce, 40

Barbecue sauce, 52

Beans, red and rice, 28

Beef
    boiled, 105
    Mahacha, 105
    pot roast, 104
    steak, smothered, 109

Biscuits, buttermilk, 7

Brussels sprouts, 115

Cabbage, fried, 240

Cake
    better than sex, 230
    chocolate sheet, 170
    coconut layer, 96
    lemon, 172
    pineapple upside-down, 70
    spice, 168

Cast iron, tips, 122

Chicken,
    fried, procedure for, 74
    salad, 186
    soup, 141

Chili, 107

Chocolate
    icing, 170
    sheet cake, 170

Cocktail franks in grape sauce, 190

Collard greens, 72

Corn bread, 90

Cream sauce, 117
    variations of, 118

Couche-couche, 92

Egg salad, 184

Flu tonic, 143

Gingersnaps, 248

Graham cracker crust, 175

Green beans, pickled, 224
Green tomatoes, fried, 22
Gumbo, seafood roux for, Ary
    Jean's, 205
Icing
    better than sex icing, 231
    caramel, 168
    chocolate, 170
    glaze, lemon, 172
Jelly, grape, 189
Key lime pie, 175
Lemon
    glaze, 172
    squares, 136
Lonely heart, remedy for, 229
Love potion, 147
Love stimulant, 228
Macaroni and cheese, 69
Mahacha, 105
Marinade
    Dell's, 250
    honey teriyaki, 234
Peas, black-eyed, 71
Pie
    key lime, 175
    lemon chess, 135
Pork roast, 110
Pot roast, Biloxi, 104
Potato(es)
    jalapeño, 116
    salad, bayou, 86
    salad, easy, 87
    salad, mashed, 85
Prosciutto and red peppers,
    xv

Roast
    pot, 104
    pork, 110
Salsa, cherry, 111
Sauce
    cocktail, 80
    grape, 190
Sandwich, fried green tomato
    and bacon, 23
Shrimp
    Alfredo, 81
    boiled, 79
    étouffée, 82
Sinking spell, remedy for, 143
Sourdough starter, 98
Steak, smothered, 109
Sugar syrup, 162
Sugared violets, 192
Sweet potato soufflé, 119
Tea
    basic procedure for iced, 158
    basic sweet tea, 163
    Mr. Coffee, iced, 158
    sugar syrup for, 162
    tipsy tea, 163
Tomatoes
    fried green, 22
    fried green, and bacon
        sandwich, 23
Tonic
    flu, 143
    lonely heart remedy, 229
    love stimulant, 228
    sinking spell, 143
Violets, sugared, 192

BOOKS BY MICHAEL LEE WEST

MAD GIRLS IN LOVE
A Novel

ISBN 0-06-098506-2 (paperback)

Michael Lee West writes about the women of Crystal Falls, Tennessee, and their men with the expertise of a down-home cook who knows just how much hot sauce to add so the cornbread isn't too sweet. Reading *Mad Girls in Love* is like settling into a chair on a porch or at the Utopian Beauty Salon—only much better.

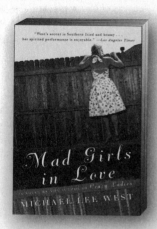

AMERICAN PIE
A Novel

ISBN 0-06-098433-3 (paperback)

"Colorful, larger-than-life characters strut and stew with zest across an equally colorful terrain . . ."
—*Kirkus Reviews*

"West is a major talent, and *American Pie* serves as proof . . . West's writing is a 'Discovery Channel' for and about people." —*Nashville Life*

CRAZY LADIES
A Novel

ISBN 0-06-097774-4 (paperback)

Though she was born in Tennessee, Miss Gussie is no country fool. A woman who can handle any situation, she has her hands full with two headstrong daughters who happen to be complete opposites. From the author of *Mad Girls in Love* comes this lively multigenerational tale of six charming, unforgettable Southern women—a novel of love and laughter, pain and redemption.

SHE FLEW THE COOP
A Novel Concerning Life, Death, Sex and Recipes in Limoges, Louisiana

ISBN 0-06-092620-1 (paperback)

Brilliantly interweaves dark calamity with comedy to depict everyday life in tiny Limoges, Louisiana, in 1952. Told through the voices of its richly eccentric characters, *She Flew the Coop* is an entrancing picture of Limoges's gossipmongering citizens and a beautifully rendered picture of small-town life, filled with wry humor and humanity.

CONSUMING PASSIONS
A Food-Obsessed Life

ISBN 0-06-098442-2 (paperback)

Laced with delicious secret recipes passed from generation to generation, *Consuming Passions* is West's delightfully quirky memoir of an adventurous food-obsessed life. By watching a multitude of relatives cook, squabble, and carry on tradition, West went from a noncooking student to a full-on gourmet of food and words. Throughout, she lends her distinctive humor and often hilarious insights to stories about her trials and tribulations as a Southern woman who became an "accidental gourmet."

"A scrumptiously witty memoir about family, food, and the American South." —*People*

"A must-read. . . . Everything about *Consuming Passions*—from the title to the recipes—just drips with Southern charm." —*Denver Post*